Praise for
This Beautiful Mess

"*This Beautiful Mess* will revolutionize the way you look at Jesus and His mission to bring the kingdom of God into our cosmos. If you are content with mere religion, don't read this book. It will force you to engage in the true mission of Christ."

> —CHRIS SEAY, pastor of Ecclesia and president
> of Ecclesia Bible Society

"Rick McKinley reveals a raw faith in *This Beautiful Mess* that will catch you off guard. He strips away the religiosity that so often shrouds the true gospel."

> —MARK BATTERSON, *New York Times* best-selling
> author of *The Circle Maker*

THIS
BEAUTIFUL
MESS

THIS
BEAUTIFUL
MESS

PRACTICING THE PRESENCE OF THE KINGDOM OF GOD

RICK McKINLEY

FOREWORD BY
DONALD MILLER

MULTNOMAH
BOOKS

THIS BEAUTIFUL MESS
PUBLISHED BY MULTNOMAH BOOKS
12265 Oracle Boulevard, Suite 200
Colorado Springs, Colorado 80921

All Scripture quotations, unless otherwise indicated, are taken from the Holy Bible, New International Version®, NIV®. Copyright © 1973, 1978, 1984 by Biblica Inc.® Used by permission of Zondervan. All rights reserved worldwide. www.zondervan.com. Scripture quotations marked (NASB) are taken from New American Standard Bible®. © Copyright The Lockman Foundation 1960, 1962, 1963, 1968, 1971, 1972, 1973, 1975, 1977, 1995. Used by permission. (www.Lockman.org).

Italics in Scripture quotations reflect the author's added emphasis.

Details in some anecdotes and stories have been changed to protect the identities of the persons involved.

Trade Paperback ISBN 978-1-60142-569-0
eBook ISBN 978-1-60142-570-6

Copyright © 2006, 2013 by Rick McKinley

Cover design by Kristopher K. Orr; cover illustration by Martin French

All contributions in the "Voices" sections of this book are written by people in the Imago Dei Community and are used by permission.

Published in the United States by WaterBrook Multnomah, an imprint of the Crown Publishing Group, a division of Random House Inc., New York.

MULTNOMAH and its mountain colophon are registered trademarks of Random House Inc.

Library of Congress Cataloging-in-Publication Data
McKinley, Rick.
    This beautiful mess : practicing the presence of the kingdom of God / by Rick McKinley with David Kopp.
        p. cm.
    Includes bibliographical references.
    1. Kingdom of God. 2. Jesus Christ—Kingdom. 3. Christian life. I. Kopp, David, 1949–
II. Title.
    BT94.M264 2006
    231.7'2—dc22

                                        2006023210

Printed in the United States of America
2013

10 9 8 7 6 5 4 3 2 1

SPECIAL SALES
Most WaterBrook Multnomah books are available at special quantity discounts when purchased in bulk by corporations, organizations, and special-interest groups. Custom imprinting or excerpting can also be done to fit special needs. For information, please e-mail SpecialMarkets@ WaterBrookMultnomah.com or call 1-800-603-7051.

To my wife, Jeanne: Your unconditional love has shown me that grace is living and breathing and embracing. You are the constant beauty in the midst of my mess.

Contents

PART 3: **PRACTICING THE PRESENCE OF THE KINGDOM**

Foreword

Years ago, I dropped off my friend John at the airport. It was early, and we'd driven for a half hour. I'd dropped John off many times before, and the drive always gave us a chance to catch up. Our conversation that morning turned to politics. The president was to visit Portland the following week, and several of my friends were joining a march they hoped would bring attention to trouble they attributed to the World Bank. As we rounded an overpass and dropped onto Airport Way, my friend said something I haven't forgotten. He said that when Jesus comes, when Jesus reigns, we will be amazed at how differently and perfectly He governs. "What do you mean?" I asked. John, who is something of a Bible scholar, provided a little more context for his comment. Jesus looked nothing like what the people of His day expected, he said. Jesus announced the arrival of the kingdom, yet He didn't work to build a government or take a stretch of land. He didn't pen a constitution. He wrote nothing, save truth and love on the hearts of His friends. That's different from any other king, living or historical. In light of this, John said, it will be interesting to see how Jesus governs.

Our conversation that morning marked the first time I had given serious consideration to the kingdom of God. Before this I'd thought of God as a shepherd, a father, a bridegroom, and so on, but not so much as a king, at least not king of an actual kingdom. I considered Him king in the way I considered Him Lord, which I'm ashamed to admit meant little more than a sentiment of praise or adoration.

What if, I began to wonder, we are actually citizens of a greater kingdom? What does that kingdom look like? How does or will Jesus govern such a kingdom? What does patriotism look like in this kingdom? And how do I really know if I am a citizen?

Growing up in the evangelical church, I heard little about the kingdom of God. If the church was doing something in the community, it was simply the local church. The church did the work, and the church took credit for the work, being careful to give ultimate glory to God. And while I considered and still consider the work of these churches to be meaningful, these actions seemed to generate from the paradigm of the church as an aid organization or community center more than as an embassy of God's kingdom. By this way of thinking, if the church had a kingdom, supported a kingdom, loved a kingdom, and defended a kingdom, that kingdom would have to be America, not some mysterious kingdom that Jesus governed.

The church I attend today, whose pastor wrote this book, embraces a different paradigm. This is not to say that we don't love America. We do. But more than America, we love the kingdom of God. Ultimately, the rules and workings of God's kingdom are a departure from the rules and workings of the utopia-envisioned declarations of our Founding Fathers. Unfortunately, their construct must balance its agenda atop the social upheaval generated by the Fall, a severe disadvantage.

Pastor Rick told me about his book before it was published. Now in its second edition, this book wonderfully clarifies some of my earlier questions regarding the mysteries of the kingdom. He also helps me understand my role in this kingdom and why Imago Dei, our church, involves itself in the world so differently than any other congregation I've been a part of.

As I read this book, I feel a sense of relief that—as tragic and temporary as the kingdoms of the world may be—true justice, true peace, true unity in diversity will happen within the kingdom of God and that this kingdom—one without borders or flags—is actually alive and active throughout the world today. Considering humankind's limited ability to demonstrate kingship (a few thousand wars come to mind), I personally find great hope in the presence of the kingdom of God and a deeper desire to participate in it.

I want to thank Rick for bringing these issues to the table and for offering us, with humor and wisdom, a view into the workings of the kingdom. I hope you enjoy this book as much as I have and find within these pages more than a perspective on the kingdom of God, but an invitation to act on behalf of a better world.

All the love of Christ to you in the process,

Donald Miller
Portland, Oregon

Preface to the Second Edition

A lot has happened over the seven years since *This Beautiful Mess* was first released. Time does that, I suppose. Gray hairs have found their way into the beard of that thirty-something pastor who seemingly overnight became a forty-something pastor. With those years came loss and pain but lots of joy as well.

The son I write about in chapter 7 is no longer thirteen but twenty-one and old enough to share a pint with me. My children have grown, as has that mustard seed that first fell into the hearts of a handful of people who called themselves Imago Dei Community. That community has morphed into something better than I had ever dreamed possible. The seed continues to grow into a beautiful tree sprouting the "already and not yet" reality that is the kingdom of God. It's a vision of love and peace and hope and new life breaking into ordinary places and making them extraordinary. I am more humbled than ever to be part of such a vision.

Perhaps more important, I am seeing that Jesus' vision of His kingdom has spread like rays of sun over the city of Portland. So many amazing things have happened that I can't take the time to tell, but perhaps a story or two will lend some validation to my claims.

Portland sits in the great Northwest as a proudly progressive city that most would say has little tolerance for the church and her ancient claims of a resurrected Savior. Over the past seven years, however, we have seen this city take notice of the people of the King, and not because of what we are *against* but what we are *for*.

On this score, a growing collective of kingdom people are leading the way. Portland has one of the worst epidemics of sex trafficking in the country. With this ugly fact in mind, the churches of Portland have collaborated with city officials from the mayor to city commissioners to the social-service agencies to make this horrific reality a memory. As part of our work together, churches have given large amounts of money to help build safe houses for victims of sex trafficking. In doing this, we have grown relationships across many lines that have led to amazing conversations about the peace, love, and hope that come from Jesus. Former victims have been rescued! The echoes of Isaiah 61 can be heard through the streets of our city: "He will set the captives free."

We have seen nonprofits emerge from this joint effort to help eradicate sex trafficking. The church has funded positions for advocates who work within the system so that more and more people are trained and available to help the many girls in need. The people of the King have volunteered as counselors to assist children in healing and recovery from such a devastating reality.

These initiatives are shaping the culture of the city as well as the conversation of the church. For example, *Christianity Today's* "This Is Our City" project made Portland its first stop. Working with the project staff was a gift, and their work is worth your time to read.

Another area in which Christ's body has made a mark is with at-risk kids. A few years ago, Portland churches gave the city one hundred thousand dollars to begin a mentoring program for the most at-risk eighth graders in the city. Five hundred of them! Along with funds, the church provided mentors for these students. The mentors stayed in touch through high school to serve as friends and expose the students to the possibilities that awaited them if they finished school. The mentors visited college campuses with them and talked about their dreams. Where there was perhaps very little hope, the kingdom broke in through flesh-and-bone relationship. God's people showed up in the love of Christ to go on a journey through the lives of these kids.

The reason for this program stemmed from a tragic fact. For more than a decade, over 40 percent of Portland's high school students dropped out. Such a high number has a cascading impact on our city. Hopeless young adults turn to dead ends such as the sex or drug industry or end up among our homeless teen population.

Then one amazing evening, I sat at a gathering of leaders and donors. Instrumental in the move of God here has been internationally known evangelist Luis Palau and his organization. That night we gathered to celebrate the story of Luis and his ministry that spans over fifty years and has impacted millions of people. Partway through the night, Sam Adams, Portland's mayor at the time, came to the stage. Sam announced that four years after the mustard seed of our little mentor dream had taken root, change had come. For the first time in fifteen years, the dropout rate had been reduced by about 15 percent! He said that this was directly related to the work of the church! A truly remarkable relationship had brought the beauty of the kingdom to the forefront of our city.

For every statistic, there is a story. Young people who didn't think they had much of a future are now dreaming of what they can become. Young people are going to college, not meth houses, heading to careers, not to Eighty-Second Avenue to sell their bodies for a meal. And perhaps most important, they have friends and mentors who love Jesus and love them.

There are hundreds of stories, and I am hopeful God will allow me to tell them in future books, but they are stories of the vision that *This Beautiful Mess* holds for you and me: A vision of a King who is loving and good and whose reign has changed everything. A vision of a new realm of activity in His power that is breaking in and yet is not without opposition. A vision desperately needed for the people of God today.

As I look out at the landscape of the church, I continue to hear conversations about how to grow it, how to do it better, how to reach the postmodern folks, how to dress it up and make it seem more relevant. The problem is this: If you start with the church, you might end with the church. If you end with the church, you may never get to the kingdom. But if you start with the kingdom, you will always get the church.

The message that rings true in our city is that if the church would simply *be* the church, then the kingdom of Jesus will be displayed. What a gift it has been to participate with God in *His* vision instead of recrafting and rebranding our own.

I am grateful that this book is being updated and rereleased and that the good people at Multnomah Books believe in its message. Foremost among them is my friend David Kopp, the executive editor. I pray that this book will continue to be a small spark in the large flame of the kingdom and that its message will help others catch the fire of Jesus and His reign.

I continue to be grateful for so many who make this kind of dreaming possible for me. Two loves have altered my life eternally. The first is my wife, Jeanne, who continues to show me what heaven's grace looks like in the beauty of her blond hair and blue eyes and in the deeper beauty of her unconditional love. The second is my King. Jesus continues to draw me into the white-hot fury of His love, inviting me to relinquish my reign for His, which tears me away from self-focused living into the freedom of relationship with the Father through the Son by the Spirit. His faithfulness defeats my every act of doubt and rebellion and proves to me over and over that nothing can separate me from His love.

There is a roughness to the journey, a wrestling that keeps me authentic. But Jesus has proven to be a most able wrestler. He triumphs over my mess with the strength of His love and the beauty of His glory.

I pray that the words you read will lead you into His unstoppable vision of another, better world, of new life breaking into ordinary places and lives and making them extraordinary.

Rick McKinley
Portland, Oregon
January 2013

PART 1

Discovering the Kingdom

When Jesus was on earth, He painted a radical vision for His followers. He called it the "kingdom of God." His kingdom is a heavenly reality that lands smack in the middle of everyday life. Even here, Jesus said—in the harshness and mess of earth—His kingdom is the way things really are. His announcement was nothing less than revolutionary. Maybe it was the clash of opposites or the paradox that Jesus' kingdom exists in parallel with many lesser kingdoms, but either way, His followers were not quick to pick up on the revolution. They longed for another world—a world without oppressors, injustice, beggars, or messes. For three years, Jesus walked among a people overcome with longing and spread the good news of His kingdom. He said that His kingdom was already happening all around them. It is a historical scene that captures my heart: God in the flesh breaking in to their world with healing spiritual authority and simple yet profound words. "The kingdom of God is near," He said. "The kingdom of God is within you."

Jesus invites us to live out the historical reality of His kingdom in our contemporary post-everything culture, but we have to face a hard truth: most followers of Jesus have grown accustomed to a spirituality that doesn't remotely resemble revolution. We call Him Lord but not King, and we've gone deaf and blind to the "whole" gospel He came to share.

Part 1 of *This Beautiful Mess* is intended to help us hear the words of Jesus again and begin to shift our affections toward Him and His brilliant vision. What we'll discover is that His radical call still goes forth today. We will realize that the empire we long to embrace is His. We will understand in a new way what it means to be human, to be forgiven, to live as disciples, to become the people of the revolution.

Beautiful, Mess

Blessed are the poor in spirit, for theirs is the kingdom of heaven.

"This beautiful mess..." A weird but intriguing statement. What can be beautiful about a mess? I remember as a kid going to the dump on Saturdays with my dad. I used to love everything about it (I know, scary). I loved pulling on leather work gloves. I loved packing the truck with all the busted junk and smelly garbage we wanted to get rid of. I loved jumping up in the cab with Dad and driving away with our load, off for another adventure into the steamy lands of Middle-earth. I loved everything about going to the dump until we got there and opened the truck door. Then love turned to fascination. Piles of junk, moldering yard debris, decaying garbage, solids turning to goo and oozing all over the place. The stench of ruin and rot hit hard, like a fist in the gut. It coated the back of your throat with acid and smoke.

If you've never been a young boy, well, it's hard to explain the appeal. Maybe it's because you know you'll come back with another gross-out story of something you saw or smelled or stepped in. One time we saw a family at a rickety picnic table eating lunch right in the middle of all that stink. Tuna salad sandwiches, chips, juice, ooze. Our family laughed about that for years.

Looking back, though, I find beauty in the experience. Not in the dump itself—I'm mostly beyond the "gross is cool" stage—but in the whole "going there with Dad" experience. I was with him. I was being useful. Dad and I were working and sweating, doing men's work together. I see now that going to the dump was beautiful *and* gross and messy.

So why would I use "beautiful mess" to define the kingdom of God? God is perfect. God is not messy. Why would His kingdom be messy?

Perhaps in this way: Think of mess as real and apparent complexity, as absolute resistance against the tidy, easy, or manageable. Think of mysterious new life growing inexplicably out of loss and decay. Think of richness in what the world casts off. Think of a boy finding family and purpose and goodness in a desolate place and in the overwhelming stink of it.

Mess like that.

Jesus said, "Blessed are the poor in spirit."

Happy are the have-nots.

Favored are the forgotten.

Beautiful is the mess.

What could He have meant? How could both ends of the statement be true? All we know is that (1) inside the dynamic of that paradox is a God-sized idea and (2) to accept one truth without the other would be to miss it completely.

Christians don't like mess much, not in our world and especially not in ourselves or our churches. Somewhere along the line, we have embraced a picture of a Jesus who would turn us into perfect people unpolluted by the world or our own sin. But He didn't. In Him we are new creations; in ourselves we are dump dwellers. Longing for our full redemption, we strive to please Him and groan in our fallenness and bask in His beauty. For whatever reason, Jesus didn't choose to instantly sanitize the whole lot of us. We often think He did, though, so we spend a lot of time running around with mops and buckets, getting ready for a bunk inspection. In our kingdoms, we begin to believe that we can fix all our messes. In Jesus' kingdom, He alone can start with our messes and accomplish something we never could have imagined. And He does.

Which brings us to beauty.

The kingdom of God is the living, breathing presence and purpose and reign of God on our planet. It's beautiful *and* irreducible. To reduce it to a seven-point outline might help you on the quiz, but it won't get you any closer to the experience. It would be like cutting up a corpse to figure out what it means to be human. Sure, you'd end up with identifiable body parts in formaldehyde and maybe a micron photograph of a neurotransmitter, but the wonder of pulsing human life would elude you. Do you think in some piece of brain you'd find clues to friendship and falling in love, learn why beach sand feels good between your toes, or what it means to be a child of God who also happens to like football, cigars, and the taste of a great Cabernet?

To be human is to live with loose ends with people and in a world of loose ends, feeling you've been made for perfection but knowing you can't get there on your own. Knowing that you've been placed here to bring a taste of something beautiful and blessed.

I love studying theology, but I've noticed that theology has little tolerance for loose ends. As the study of God, it mostly uses human tools like logic and interpretation and systems to define Him and how He works in our lives. Countless brilliant women and men have written penetrating works that help us think more clearly about God. They give us a rich theological heritage, and I encourage you to read them. But be careful. You can study God expertly in His parts and miss Him entirely in

His Being. Sometimes I think today's evangelicals have dissected God, put Him in jars, labeled all His parts, and then breathed a sigh of relief. "Whew. Job done," they gasp. "Now we have no more confusion about God. Now we have a God we can market. At least now we can be excruciatingly confident that 'our team' is right."

As right as body parts in formaldehyde.

I've found that theology, especially the systematic kind, becomes more helpful when you think of it as grammar. Grammar helps us to read and write, but it cannot on its own give us one memorable sentence. That's because grammar is a tool, not an end in itself. Meaningful communication is the end for which the writer strives. Communication like, for example, poetry. Yes, grammar helps us understand and experience a poem. But just when we get comfortable, a good poet will break a language rule, turn an image inside out, give us the slip, send us falling.

There's nothing we can say in response but, "Hmm, good poem. I felt those words."

To help us encounter truths that would die if put into jars, Jesus showed us His kingdom in a gallery of poems, or word pictures. Each time, He showed us another facet of what He wanted to teach. What He did not do was give us just *one* picture of His kingdom, much less a short dictionary definition. Of course, He could have. He could have dissected it for us—defined and dead—for all to inspect.

Instead, He gave us a multifaceted picture that is full of shape and contour and texture and tension and beauty and mess. It is both three dimensional and experiential. To be known, this picture must be desired, received, and lived over and over again. In the genius of Jesus, we find ourselves grasping aspects of the kingdom through a *living* definition that is growing and changing all the time. Not neat (that's dogma). Not reduced (that's formula). Not disassembled (that's dead).

But beautiful.

In high school, my friends and I befriended one of the school employees. She was a gruff middle-aged woman. Her stern exterior was meant to scare us into good behavior, I suppose. But inside she was very cool. Like your friend's mom who was cool. That's how she was. She made sure no one left campus at lunch or smoked behind the backstops. For some reason that I still can't figure out, she really liked my group of friends. We even called her Mom.

Once, we talked Mom into going into the janitor's office and calling the school and pretending to be our moms to get us permission slips out of school. Yes, the dreaded "cutting class" ploy. I'm passing on a little personal history here, not making a recommendation (although if you didn't cut class even once, you know you wish you had). Mom made calls for three or four of us. How she pulled it off I don't know, but sure enough, while we were sitting in class, the phone rang, and the teacher sent us on our way.

Freedom! We piled into my car and made our escape. Gone, away, free. Everyone else was back in class, grinding it out, watching the clock. But we were flying, no longer prisoners of any program, rule, or schedule.

I hope this book feels like a permission slip from Mom for you: get out of religion free. You see, Someone knows and really likes you. Someone *wants* you to find that larger, freer experience of being that you sense is out there just waiting for you to live it.

I realize that seeking the King with mostly pictures and stories to go by may feel dangerous or rebellious to you. But I encourage you to receive this book not as the last theological word on anything, but as a well-intentioned, God-loving invitation to go and grow and be where you haven't been before.

Listen to the teachings of Jesus with me. Puzzle over His pictures and stories. Then look for His redemptive reign at work in the mess of your day. It's there, I promise. You may not end up with a perfect argument for every question about Jesus our King. But by the end, you'll know what it means to say, maybe for the first time, "Hmm, I feel His beauty."

Voices

Look Up Anyway

Last Wednesday I walked home as the sun came down over the Willamette. I was listening to Elliott Smith as I paced the streets of his city, wondering if he'd walked where my feet were falling, if he knew any of the people who smiled at me as I passed. It was still warm enough for my Irish skin to bear exposure. It smelled like summer and youth and hope in a way America does best at that denim blue hour of the evening. Portland is not an easy winter city. The rain washes over everything until you feel your very self eroding down to the marrow. It is a city of sodden Converse trainers, bad-hair weeks, and broken people. I was remembering riding the bus on Eighty-Second a few months ago. The most broken people in all the world ride the TriMet on Eighty-Second. They look at their feet and carry their worlds in plastic bags. They have crazy Jerry Springer hair and ill-fitting clothes. They never smile. They are not funny crazy like the people on the Burnside buses. They are sad crazy. The bus was full of these folk, and above them, pinned to the side of the bus, was a short poem:

> I believe in myself slowly
> It takes all the doubt I have
> It takes my wonder.

If it was not so sad, I would have laughed at the irony: forty people on a bus who never look up to see the only thing they need to be told.

Last Wednesday, as I padded the streets, I was thinking about this and about how Portland seems different to me now. When I think of Portland, I think of beauty pushing through brokenness. I think of individual people and their intricate grace stories emerging from the ugliness. I think of community and art and freedom, individuality, color, music, culture, and diversity all laughing loud in adversity's face. On the side of a falling-down building at the bottom of Belmont, someone has painted the cutest little flower and in spidery handwriting has crowned it with the commandment "Take a Stand." This is Portland to me. It's about buying back the ugliness and redeeming it for a better purpose. It's about acknowledging that sometimes you cannot change your situation, yet choosing to look up anyway and stare hope straight in the eye.

—Jan Carson

What If?

> The kingdom of heaven is like treasure hidden in a field.

You're flying back from Denver, and sitting next to you on the plane is a gentleman in a bright red robe with a fluffy collar. While you wait for your peanuts, you make small talk. You find out the guy is from a small Asian country.

"Yeah, I think I've heard of it," you say, but of course you're just being polite. What you really want to know is, *What's with the outfit?*

"Fascinating," you say, trying to keep things going. "So what do you do there?"

"I rule there," he replies matter-of-factly. "It's my country—all of it. You see, I'm the king."

"You're kidding," you say. A pretty lame response, you immediately realize, but, well, you've never met a royal anyone before, much less sat next to a king on an airplane.

"No. It's true," he says.

The peanuts arrive. It takes a little munching in silence before you can come up with a next line.

"Fascinating," you finally say. Lame again. But you plunge ahead. "So that explains the, uh, robe and all."

"Yes, these are my travel clothes."

More munching. You're wondering about the guy's throne clothes.

Finally, "You wouldn't happen to also have a crown, would you?" you ask.

"Yes, but not with me. I wear it when I am ruling. I don't rule on this airplane."

And that's when it hits you. As impressed as you are with your imperial seatmate, on this plane he's pretty much just another guy. He's a king, okay, but his kingdom is not where you live, so his reign has no practical effect on your life. He can't order you around, expect you to bow, pardon you from something you did wrong—all the usual king stuff. Not here anyway. Here he's just a nice guy eating peanuts. A nice guy with a cool title in a fluffy red outfit.

You smile and sit back. This is great. And you're going home with a killer story.

A couple of hours later, you walk off the plane and back onto the wonderful terra firma of your own personal democracy. One me, one vote. Life, liberty, and the all-American pursuit of my whatever.

Ah, home.

But what if...

What if the ground you touched turned out not to be yours? And the air and all beings and all lesser powers—they weren't yours either? What if you stepped off that plane into an actual kingdom, a place and time under the dominion of a sovereign Lord who *did* rule from horizon to horizon whether you bowed to Him or not, whether you knew He existed or not?

It could happen. I think it already did.

One day a messenger from God stood on a hillside surrounded by a crowd of sweaty, hungry, desperate people—men, women, old people, young lovers, kids. As He looked into their eyes, He saw a question: "Are you the One?" And behind the question He saw longing. Longing for "the One" to come and explain why the world was such a wreck. Longing for rescue, for healing, for one moment of insight that would change it all. Longing for their one true King to show up and reclaim His kingdom and kick the Roman occupiers out and make everything right again.

Jesus looked into their eyes—eyes full of longing—and told them stories.

> The kingdom of heaven is like yeast that a woman took and mixed into a large amount of flour until it worked all through the dough.

> The kingdom of heaven is like a mustard seed, which a man took and planted in his field. Though it is the smallest of all your seeds, yet when it grows, it is the largest of garden plants and becomes a tree, so that the birds of the air come and perch in its branches.

> The kingdom of heaven is like treasure hidden in a field. When a man found it, he hid it again, and then in his joy went and sold all he had and bought that field.

I think they listened to every word out there in the hot sun. The kingdom, He was saying, is powerful, invasive, unbelievably beautiful. The kingdom is waiting to be discovered in the dirt of their everyday lives. And it is a prize worth everything. Everything.

With each story, they were thinking, *Yes, yes, that's it. That's exactly what we want. Could it be true? And could He...be the One?*

And I think their longing deepened.

For the next three years, Jesus laid out His gospel. Speaking in homes, on roadsides, from boats, in synagogues, He spread the good news of the kingdom. *Kingdom* they understood. After all, they lived in a world defined by kings and emperors. Some of His hearers listened and believed. Some turned away.

We can hear for ourselves what Jesus said. We have an ancient, reliable text that God has graciously preserved over two thousand years so that we, too, can hear the stories and claim the treasure and become joyful participants in a world where Christ is King. A very real kingdom that Jesus came to announce remains, its reality carried forward in a rich tradition of kingdom people down through the history of the church.

The news of the kingdom was, in fact, the primary message of Jesus. Think of it as what God came to earth to say. In Matthew it is called "the kingdom of heaven" and is referred to thirty-one times. In Luke and elsewhere the subject comes up sixty-five times as "the kingdom of God." In the book of Acts, disciples like Peter, Stephen, and Paul took it as their whole mission to preach the good news of the kingdom of God *and* salvation in the name of Jesus Christ. Both.

Interestingly, in the rest of the New Testament, the writers don't appear to have any need to rehash or defend Jesus' teachings. They simply accept them as true and set about to proclaim what He proclaimed. To them His message was the most complete description available of a new way of being human and alive. Those first-century believers put on the kingdom gospel like a new set of glasses, saw everything differently from that day on, and never took them off.

Things are different for most followers of Jesus now, though. We say we follow Jesus and put Him first in our lives. But look at how Western

Christians live and think and what we aspire to. When you observe what passes for American Christianity—in politics, on Christian television, in churches, across our editorial pages—don't you sometimes find yourself saying, "I don't want to join that team"?

Honestly, I think we're more like that guy getting off the plane. We take the "Jesus is our Savior" message home like a really good story, but Jesus as King has no place in our lives. Kings are for fairy tales and burger commercials. Kings wear funny clothes and funny hats. We don't need a king. What we need, we think, is a little more defense of our doctrines and a little more time to tidy up our messes. That's all we need, and then our world will go better.

Except it doesn't. And though we'll keep trying until the day we drop (like good little Christians do), we can't quite explain why.

God stood before us in human shoes and told stories one after another of what His kingdom is really like. He told us why it's really here and how much it's really worth. He showed us who He really is. But like many in Christ's day, we have turned away, leaving behind impressive opinions like "profound moral teaching" and "He should be in the White House" and "beautiful but obviously impossible" and "Won't the world be great when everyone else is left behind and just us Jesus folks remain?"

We have taken His free salvation insurance like those folks on the hillsides ate His free lunches. Then we go home. We carry with us a nice Jesus with a cool title. But all the same, we go home King-less.

But what if Jesus was never meant to be separated from His kingdom? Not then, not now, not ever? What if God broke into our world back then with a revolutionary message of truth, life, and freedom that His followers today have parted out, like an old '57 Chevy up on blocks, keeping just a few of the shinier parts?

What if we have run off with the Teacher's sheet music, squabbling over every note, but have never actually heard His symphony?

Jesus' kingdom invites us to immerse ourselves in the whole gospel He came to preach. We get to listen and consider and think through the staggering possibilities of kingdom living as Jesus taught it. The practical promise of our faith journey together is this: as we live in fidelity to Christ the King, His in-breaking reign will have a transformational effect on us, our communities, and our world. Anything less is not what Jesus came to earth to tell.

In a mysterious yet absolutely real way, the kingdom of Jesus *is* here now and in power. Like gravity or high-frequency radio waves, this kingdom doesn't require our attention or consent in order to exist. It just is. Still, I think you'll find that we have to learn—and deeply want—to see and imagine in new ways. Otherwise we'll miss it. So many have.

Because it is like a treasure buried.

Voices

Rahab's Song

in the dirt i used to kneel
idols fixed upon vain hopes
blocks of wood brought down with weight
    of prayers spilled
but you came and stole my heart
now i pray to ears unstopped
i am watched over by eyes i can't outrun

you are God alone
lesser gods before you scatter
to the winds like sand
for you, the God i love
i lay down my broken idols
following your steps

i can feel upon my skin
that your tears have met with mine
and the earth around me shakes with your
       resolve
all my hope in you i find
all my heart like water poured
what is one more drop in hands that frame
       the world?

—Vania Moore

Harpooning God

> Jesus traveled about from one town and
> village to another, proclaiming the good news
> of the kingdom of God.

I spent many years not knowing what Jesus meant when He used the terms *kingdom of God* and *kingdom of heaven*. I simply dismissed the terms as something related to the afterlife. When I became a Christ follower, the sad truth is that I transferred Christ into *my* kingdom, into the context of *my* life. My kingdom consisted of my desires and aspirations, namely, the future I hoped for, an agenda that allowed me to reign as I chose. It all sounds selfish. It was and it still is. Thinking back, I believe I had no category in my life through which to comprehend the kingdom of God. For eighteen years I had lived my own life and served myself. I assumed that sooner or later other people would realize the great reality of me. Of course, they'd then hop on the bandwagon and serve me too.

I wasn't good at ruling my little kingdom, though. I ended up a failed king with a broken life. That's when Jesus did indeed break into my life. He accepted me as is, brokenness and all. He forgave my truckload of sins. Life was new.

I quickly put Jesus into service.

I learned, of course, the appropriate language to assure everyone that I was serving Him. Probably it was an ugly mix of the old and the new. I was serving Him, wanting to live my life for Him, but not too much. I still wanted to be in charge. Plus I held this amazing new grace card that let me get out of jail free.

Eventually my spiritual bubble burst. I realized that Jesus did not want to help me be a better king. Neither did He want to be king of *my* kingdom. Really, I was a lot like those patriotic crowds in Palestine who wanted Him to be king of their country. I was simply trying to get God to endorse my agenda. But He would have none of it.

At the time it felt like a crisis. God seemed to be stepping away from me, almost abandoning me. I was unsure what the problem was. Had God quit liking me? Didn't He appreciate the plans I was making for the two of us?

I took matters into my own hands. There's a wealth of information about how to get God back on track, you know. Go to any Christian bookstore. You'll find seven steps to the perfect life, quick fixes for deeper spirituality, self-help plans for godliness, success, health, wealth… All for God's glory, of course. All written by deep, successful people with expensive teeth. Those books danced around like magic pills just waiting for me to swallow.

In the end, though, Jesus still would have none of it. I ended up with lots of books that didn't work, cluttering my shelves, and a lot of money gone.

But at least it was a beginning. I realize now that God was not abandoning me. He just wanted nothing to do with my kingdom agenda. First, we had to settle the kingdom dilemma. Had Jesus bowed to my agenda, He would not have been the true God. Instead of being in relationship with the living, untamable, dangerously loving God of Scripture who graciously made Himself known to me through His Son, Jesus, I would have gone away with little more than an imaginary pet.

If you set out right now to tell the story of your encounters with the King of heaven, I wonder what you would say. What foolish tantrums and ugly battles could you describe as you think about how you have tried to get God to serve your kingdom?

Our vast capacity for personal autonomy is actually just one reason the gospel of Jesus so often gets set aside. The other big one is that the gospel of Jesus is difficult.

Perhaps no other New Testament teaching has been so argued about by so many down through the centuries. We read the pages of Matthew, Mark, Luke, and John, and we puzzle. For example, the core of Jesus' gospel seems to be that the kingdom is arriving: "The kingdom of God is at hand," He says. But what does this mean? At times Jesus speaks of the kingdom as something present that we can experience now: "The kingdom of God is within you." Other times He speaks of the kingdom coming on the clouds at the end of time.

Well, which is it?

Plenty of thinkers have tried to make all of Jesus' teachings stand up straight and line up right. Problem is, we don't understand kingdom language, so we don't know what in the world Jesus is talking about most of the time. We've ended up with a lot of pre-, post-, and a-systematic theology that has created divisions among the followers of Jesus.

On the issue of Jesus' gospel of the kingdom, theologians have tended to take one of several approaches. For example:

- They *reduce* the gospel of the kingdom: it's just the church.
- They *spiritualize* the gospel of the kingdom: it's completely realized now.

- They *postpone* the gospel of the kingdom: it will only be realized in heaven.

Ultimately, these attempts come off as convenient but somewhat man-centered. Without intending to, they take away the full promise and impact of Jesus' teachings.

Jesus' kingdom teaching *is* challenging. No doubt. It doesn't present the kind of meaningful measurements Western minds expect. Maybe that's why we'd rather systematize and recover some sense of control than live by what has proven to be hard. Even if Jesus preached it.

But consider the consequences of accepting a Savior while rejecting the King.

On a personal level, we inevitably fall victim to ourselves (failed rulers, all). A self-based faith leads to dysfunction and disillusionment. For example, I've noticed that when things go wrong in my King-less kingdom, I'm often arrogant enough to blame God for my trouble. That's because my worldview is warped to begin with, so I end up twisting truths I "know" in order to support my own rule. Here's another example: I start thinking—very piously, mind you—that Jesus is the answer for all my temporal problems. Problems like money, health, career, and relationships. Yet where did He promise that? (What He actually said was, "In this world you will have trouble.") But when our lives are all about us, the appeal of that kind of bumper-sticker dumbness is irresistible. "Christ in you, the hope of glory" gets turned into an assurance of our business successes instead of a promise that brings peace to our souls when all hell breaks loose.

At the community level, we see King-less errors creeping in all the time, twisting how Christians think and live and bringing dishonor to God. Take, for example, televangelists who trot out a Bible verse and tell you that God wants you to be rich, but somehow the whole get-rich system that "God created" requires that you send *them* money. Well, it works for them. It doesn't seem to occur to them that Jesus was a former carpenter turned homeless preacher. Perhaps Jesus didn't know how the system worked.

Here's the bottom line: even the best theologian in the world cannot get a kingdom-less God to work. Neither can you or I. We may feel that we harpooned Him long ago, but now we can't seem to figure out how to fillet Him. Every time we try, He jumps off the table.

We end up living in a sea of chaos, where Jesus' kingdom people are chasing after anything that will get Him to work His magic on their behalf. In other words, get the King to serve the bricklayers and barmaids.

From personal experience I can tell you that He *will* let you live in your own construct, if you choose. But He'll *never* bow down to you or adapt Himself to your beliefs.

I'm grateful for that.

How, then, do we begin to make sense of any of this? What could our lives look like if we took up Jesus' invitation to reorient our lives to His kingdom revolution? What if we really took Him as our King and submitted to His rule? What if we organized our lives to be faithful to His kingdom's culture?

What if…

PART 2

Re-Visioning Life in the Kingdom

Once we gain an understanding of what the kingdom of God is, we need to know where to look for it. "I'm ready to see the kingdom messages of Jesus in a new light," you might be saying, "but where is His kingdom in my life now? I just don't see it." To recognize the kingdom, we need to learn to see differently. Not just see differently in a theoretical sense, but in a real-world sense. Like when sin and brokenness and a world gone wrong show up on our doorsteps. See the kingdom breaking in there too. That's what part 2 of *This Beautiful Mess* is about. For most of us, it will take some effort to reorient our thinking and expectations toward the new reality that Jesus came to announce. In fact, since most of us have been imagining a King-less world for years, a certain amount of deprogramming will probably be involved. But after we leave some comfortable assumptions behind, we'll be ready to grapple in new and healing ways with our culture and the relentless demands it places on us to make a destiny for ourselves apart from God.

In doing so, we'll begin to see what we've overlooked before: His present kingdom in the midst of the ordinary miracle in which we live.

Seeing Through

> Jesus went into Galilee, proclaiming the good news of God. "The time has come," he said. "The kingdom of God is near. Repent and believe the good news!"

Look out your window. Where is the kingdom of God? You see high-rises. A lady walking her schnauzer in a red sweater (that is, the dog wearing the sweater). A magnolia tree in bloom. A taxi parked by the curb, the driver's cigarette smoke rising from the window like a pale blue scarf. A jet overhead taking your son or daughter to war. Over and over, Jesus said His kingdom was near, very near. So near that it's here. But where? If it's anywhere, how do you actually see it? Go back with me to that hillside crowd listening to the rabbi from Nazareth. They were there because Jesus had launched His ministry with a startling two-sentence sermon: "The kingdom of God is near. Repent and believe the good news!" Those two sentences, I believe, are the best place for us to start if we want to get our eyesight back. Let me try to explain.

When the people of Jesus' day heard Him say, "The kingdom of God is at hand," they had a closer idea of what He meant. They understood that as God-fearing Jews they were part of a chosen family, a spiritual and physical nation whose temple and throne were both in Jerusalem. Of course, for the last five hundred years or so, things had not gone well for either the monarchy or the spirit. But still, they believed the promise God had sent through the prophets: one day His literal reign over all the earth would be restored. People wrote and sang spiritual songs about the moment. It was part of Israel's story.

Longing for the return of the King filled their dreams and songs. Take a minute to appreciate these worship lyrics from Psalm 47:

> Clap your hands, all you nations;
>> shout to God with cries of joy.
> How awesome is the LORD Most High,
>> the great King over all the earth!
> He subdued nations under us,
>> peoples under our feet.
> He chose our inheritance for us,
>> the pride of Jacob, whom he loved.

And these from Psalm 96:

> Say among the nations, "The LORD reigns."
>> The world is firmly established, it cannot be
>>> moved;
>> he will judge the peoples with equity.
> Let the heavens rejoice, let the earth be glad;
>> let the sea resound, and all that is in it;
>> let the fields be jubilant, and everything in
>>> them.

Then all the trees of the forest will sing for joy;
> they will sing before the LORD, for he comes,
> he comes to judge the earth.
He will judge the world in righteousness
> and the peoples in his truth.

These songs clearly describe what devout Jews anticipated. They expected an actual reign by an actual king. Their king would bring tangible changes: freedom from oppressors, and justice and dignity for all peoples. The world would finally know the one true God. People would cry out for joy. The biosphere would erupt in singing. Literally!

But best of all, the King of heaven Himself would finally be physically *with them,* not just listening to their prayers or hiding in their laws or hovering above them in the smoke of their sacrifices. But walking their streets. Talking in their markets. Leading their army. Here's how the prophet Zechariah announced it:

"Shout and be glad, O Daughter of Zion. For I am coming, and I will live among you," declares the LORD. "Many nations will be joined with the LORD in that day and will become my people. I will live among you and you will know that the LORD Almighty has sent me to you."

I imagine that those folks on the hillside listening to the rabbi Jesus tell stories about pearls and weeds and seeds were asking themselves, *Could He be the One who is to come? This Jesus, a son of suspicious circumstances? This wandering healer and teacher? This kin to that bug-eating John the Baptist? Are You the One?*

For three years the nation put those questions to Him in a hundred ways.

Pretty much, their conclusion was, *No way.*

Interesting, isn't it? They had decent motives. They had their biblical learning lined up. They even had the evidence of miracles. But when they got to the King Himself, they were blind. Yes, they believed in the *idea* of the kingdom of God, but the *person* of Jesus didn't meet their expectations. They saw not a king but a bad risk, and they rejected Him.

With vision like that, they might as well have been looking for a lunatic or a schnauzer in a sweater.

For us, the King is near—always. But the King and His kingdom are just not what we expect. If we trust our own assumptions, no matter how historically or religiously correct, we'll miss Him too. We'll be as blind as they were.

I think that's why one of the first words out of the mouth of the visiting King was this: "Repent."

Repent is a word we're not terribly stoked about in our culture. It might be just one notch above *STD* or the phrase *You're fired.* We picture it on a sign in a *New Yorker* cartoon. We hear it from some angry, red-faced guy shouting at us from across the street. His spit flies out into the oncoming traffic. He's dragging a fifteen-foot cross through the crowd. People can't wait to get past him. It's sad, really, that a wild-eyed street preacher is stealing the beauty of Christ's message. (I wonder if the preacher knows that.)

But what if Jesus said "repent" in a completely different way? For example, imagine that He is looking you in the eye right now and speaks the word.

"Repent," He says, smiling, confident.

"Repent."

His eyes tell you that He knows you well. His tone of voice hints that one day you'll see that repenting was the best choice you ever made. His body language exudes so much positive energy that you get the sense He might have come halfway around the world just to tell you the news. "Repent."

If you heard it like that, you would receive the word as a gift. It still might not sound like good news, but in the long run, you would find that it was.

To repent means to turn around, to stop what you're doing and do the opposite. To repent means that even though you assumed one thing was true, you now know it's wrong—all wrong—and you will now believe and act upon something totally different. *Repent* is a good, strong word, full of hope and new beginnings. In the context of Jesus' kingdom, repent is an invitation to another world, another life, a way of being that was supposed to be all along and can be now.

If we want with all our hearts to see and experience the kingdom that Jesus came to announce, we must begin with the promise of His first word. We must turn around. Go the opposite way. That one small human act invites a spiritual, wholly divine response. There's no other way to break through our natural limitations and experience the kingdom of Jesus.

Actually, we need to repent often. We need to repent, for example, of our convenient assumption that following Jesus and pursuing the American Dream are in complete harmony and will take us in pretty much the same direction. They won't. The reality of the kingdom is dangerous and beautiful and life altering.

We need to repent of smugly held beliefs, especially the so-called enlightened ones that convince us we have no need to repent. We need to repent of our rightness, our arrogant belief that since we care about goodness—for example, we see genocide for the evil it is—we'll see every evil for what it is, including the evil hiding in our own hearts.

Repentance means that we choose to agree only with God's perspective. That He alone *is* God and He alone understands the blatant ways in which our own hearts deceive us. Evil that we will never notice exists in us and around us, yet it's as obvious to God as genocide is to us.

To repent is to say to God: "I'm blind. I *don't* see, but I want to. Please show me Your heart in everything."

One of the biggest challenges to following Jesus into His kingdom is not a lack of direction but a lack of desire. Most of us don't really want to do it.

When the Imago Dei Community numbered only about twenty and we were still meeting in a borrowed basement, it became apparent to me that this was our problem. We didn't "want to," but not because we didn't understand what God was calling us to. What part of loving your enemies or embracing a child is confusing? We knew what to do, but we couldn't bring ourselves to act.

We realized that if we wanted to live out the kingdom, we would need to get our hearts before God. Only His Spirit can create spiritual desire. As pastor, I couldn't make anyone in our little group, let alone myself, want the kingdom. We needed God to change us.

One night in the borrowed church, I announced that we would start meeting each Wednesday night to repent and pray for Portland (not the coolest thing to invite your friends to). I printed out lists of every need I could think of in the city. The next Wednesday evening, we sat in a circle and prayed about those things. We had just enough desire to show up, pray, and get honest—and that's what we told God.

Things got honest real fast. "I hate my neighbor," one person prayed. "I don't think I love You, God," said another. We told God that we wanted to care but didn't, not really. We told Him we were afraid to follow Him completely because we didn't want to look like idiots. We didn't want to risk losing our comforts. Of course, we were confessing realities most of us knew, but we'd been *just good enough* church folk not to say them aloud.

Week after week in that basement, we prayed for Portland and told God the truth about our own hearts. For six months we prayed. *Will anything ever change?* I wondered. *Am I failing as a church planter?* Bit by bit, degree by degree, we hauled on the steering wheel of our spiritual ship and waited to see what God would do.

Gradually something happened. I felt it. We all did. Something in us was turning. For the first time, we were experiencing an authentic "want to." No gimmicks or games or seven steps. No flashy programs. But with God's help, we were beginning to embark on a new way of being and of seeing the world.

A new way like socks and cigarettes, for example.

Christian and Joy and others in our group started passing out socks and cigarettes to the street youth of Portland. Hundreds of kids living on the streets were confronted with the kingdom through socks and cigarettes. The socks and cigarettes met needs, spoke their language, announced that someone cared, and showed them that no one is a throwaway in the kingdom of heaven.

Socks and cigarettes are just one of the stories to come out of those early times at Imago Dei (more stories to come in the chapters ahead). True desire for the in-breaking reign of Jesus started showing up in many simple and profound ways. We didn't have a clue about what to do or how to do it, but we were finally turned around and heading in the right direction.

I believe it all started because we took Jesus' invitation to heart. He said, "Repent," and we said, "Yes."

I'm glad Jesus wasn't a politician, telling us what we wanted to hear or selling us the same old crap that never works. I am grateful for His honesty and truth. He invites us to take courage, to believe that the kingdom of God *is* the good news we've been waiting for and to realize that without a radical turning of the heart, we'll never be able to see what He is doing in our world and is inviting us to be part of.

So much of repentance is about dying to old things and inviting new life into the new things of the Spirit. Imago Dei had to ask the hard question: Do we actually want the revolution of Jesus to break into our lives and our community? Frankly, we were worried about what we might lose.

I have told our story to many church leaders. The weird thing is that most of them smile and get excited and inspired, but nothing changes because they try to do kingdom stuff without a desire for the King. In short, they never repent. Repenting turns us away from our own poverty and toward God's best. His kingdom is here among us. It is moving and accessible. Why miss it?

To His followers who were afraid to trust that God would provide for them, Jesus said:

> Seek first his kingdom and his righteousness, and all these things
> will be given to you as well.

What if you found your own borrowed basement—any place where in solidarity with others you could seek first His kingdom and His righteousness? What if you started praying for the things around you that break His heart, even if they don't yet break yours? Ask Him to show you the obvious needs you've been missing. Tell God the truth about your fears and desires.

Wait on Him and hold on for the turning.

Voices

We Are a People

we are a people.
we are a people
loved but left
alone we all fell
apart, by big strokes
and all our eyes that told of big hopes and
             wasted lives
fell on Jesus
who caught us
like knives.

and even now he makes us a people.

—Caleb Kytonen

5

A Dimension of Being

> He told them another parable: "The kingdom
> of heaven is like a mustard seed, which a man
> took and planted in his field. Though it is the
> smallest of all your seeds, yet when it grows,
> it is the largest of garden plants and becomes
> a tree, so that the birds of the air come and
> perch in its branches."
>
> He told them still another parable: "The
> kingdom of heaven is like yeast that a woman
> took and mixed into a large amount of flour
> until it worked all through the dough."

I have spent my life trying to get to the next level. You work hard and save money so you can get through school, buy a better car, buy a house, have kids. But every level requires that you try to get to the next level. Your new job requires a better car. Your children require a bigger house. Your bigger house requires a better job and longer hours. And so the cycle goes. We're like salmon swimming upstream to spawn, trying to get up the next rapids, the next fish ladder. Each time we beat the current and jump to the next level, another level is waiting.

Spiritually we tend to think in levels too. Everything depends on what we *do.*

When I first became a Christ follower, I was invited to a Bible study. I worked with a great guy who loved on me and taught me the Bible as we worked through a little study book. I ate it up. I wanted to show him how seriously I was really taking this. When we finished the first book, he mentioned there was a second one in the series that we should go through.

Bring it on, I thought. I was all for it. I devoured that one and soon moved on to the next, then the next one, and the next one after that.

One day I got tired of little study books. I wondered what number I would be working on in ten years. I had thought that getting to the next level would get me to a deeper spiritual life. I wanted to get that "deeper spiritual life" thing done and taken care of, then move on to new business. But there was no end to it. All I ever arrived at was a new level that needed reaching.

You might recognize yourself in my spiritual striving or you might not. But I see that kind of striving and competitiveness everywhere: in our free-market economy, in our relationships and career plans, in our fitness programs, in our churches.

Churches especially. Pastors and lay leaders love to talk about advancing the kingdom, building the kingdom. It's as if Jesus said, "My kingdom is a pile of lumber on the truck in heaven, and I need you boys and girls to get a hammer and help Me nail this thing together. Could ya?"

But He didn't. When Jesus talked about the kingdom, He never talked about our building it or advancing it. Never. He said, "The kingdom is…" He simply invited His followers to see it, embrace it, believe in the unfading reality of it, and join in what His Father was already doing in the world.

Being kingdom people. I love that and I hate it.

I love it because it implies some sort of discovery that I am going to have to make to truly understand what Jesus is talking about. But *being* before *doing* is not in my makeup. *Doing,* for one thing, requires more of me. Therefore *doing* adds immediately to my sense of self-importance. I think that is why I hate *being.*

Ask any leader. *Doing* is a much easier objective to rally the troops around than *being.* How many messages have you heard telling you that God is calling us to simply *be* in His kingdom? Nothing to do, buy, sign up for, build. Nowhere to prove yourself. Not many, I'm guessing.

By contrast, what if I told you that the world is broken and that *we* are God's answer to the world's problems? Well, perhaps you'd pay attention then. You yourself—and all that you can do—are crucial to the future of the planet. Just like you secretly and humbly expected all along.

Of course, it's not true. The kingdom *is.* That's it. Jesus does not need you or me to nail anything together.

Kind of throws me off. I like thinking in terms of levels of achievement, because it gives me a sense of power and control. I mean, if I work hard and do the right things, I can move to the next level. There's not so much ambiguity or mystery to the process of making God work for me. All I need to know is what the next level is and what I need to do to get there.

The other reason I like levels is that they require less of me relationally. Levels of spirituality are perfect for a culture that deifies individuals. Our world is focused on self; the kingdom is about the *other.* The kingdom demands that I notice others, love others, pray for them, and serve them. "Levels spirituality" does not. It allows me to do it myself and by myself.

Jesus hates levels spirituality. All it does is reinforce the lie that started way back in the beginning, the one that says we can be like God. How screwed up have we gotten that we cling to a Christianity that can be lived without God?

Pretty screwed up.

I am a church planter, which simply means that I started my church. At Imago Dei Community, we started from nothing and have grown to be a decent-sized little church. I also help to train and coach other church planters as they start their churches.

You know what makes a church planter depressed on a Monday morning? Low attendance or a low offering the day before. If the poor pastor happens to get hit by both, he may need to be put on suicide watch.

For the person attending a young church, the perspective is different. Let's say that person is you. This week you decide to go to church. But come next Sunday you decide not to. You have a birthday party to deal with. Or a relative to visit. A bunch of friends are going snowboarding. Real-life stuff. Anyway, you think your church decision is yours to make and no one else really cares.

But someone—the pastor—cares, and I am sad to admit it's not always about your spiritual well-being, although that concern is down there somewhere. Nickels and noses. Levels. That's what makes or breaks Sundays for most people starting a church.

I remember one Sunday when we were first starting out. We had about thirty people. We met on Sunday evenings in a Baptist church that was kind enough to rent us space cheap. That particular Sunday also happened to be the seventh game of the NBA championship, and Portland was playing L.A. for the title. As you can guess, I was in for a kick in the groin.

We sat in a darkened room with candles lit. Seemed like an artistic, atmospheric thing to do. But when I stood up to preach to twelve young women who didn't care if Portland won or lost or that Portland even has an NBA team, it felt more like a funeral held by a bunch of sorority sisters whose cat had been hit by a car.

That night we slid from thirty to twelve, and even though rationally I could tell you why our turnout was low, my heart was reeling. Here I was, trying to jump to the next attendance level, and our church had slid.

A 60 percent drop in one week. Where was God? What did I do wrong? Why were we both failing?

I am not proud of my reaction.

The problem didn't stop when we started growing either. Our numbers rose to two hundred, then to four hundred, then to six hundred and up. But on any given Sunday, that cold fear of falling behind in the levels, of failing at the numbers game, can still creep up on me. How can I allow church—a community that was created to be a place where Christ loves, heals, and redeems—to be reduced to a place where I am defined by numbers?

At the root of so much of that desire is pride, covetousness, a need for control, and self-centered striving. Sin, in other words. I have repented of that and probably will again next Monday.

To hell with the levels.

That is basically what Jesus has to say about it. Of course, it's not that He doesn't want communities of believers to grow and have influence. But there's no ladder. There's nothing we need to do to make the kingdom happen at Imago. No day will come when we'll get to the top and receive our gold star. Why?

Because there is no top.

My friend Clint was a church planter in the Bahamas. Just in case you're going to judge his motives, you should know that Clint was born and raised there. He tells a story about the day an eighteen-year-old kid dropped by his church a few years ago and changed Clint's life:

> I hear this knock on my office door, and I look up. A young man says, "Hey, Pastor Clint, can I talk to you?" I recognize this kid. He's Solomon from the car-wash stand in the parking lot.

"Pastor, God told me to tell you something," he says.

A few thoughts run through my head, but I decide to humor him, "Okay, Solomon," I say. "I have a few minutes to hear a word from God."

"Pastor Clint," he says, "you know what the difference is between a dimension and a level?"

"No, I don't," I say. So Solomon proceeds to explain the difference. Honestly, what he is saying makes no sense to me whatsoever.

"Now do you understand the difference?" he asks.

"No, not really," I say as kindly as possible.

"That's okay. God said you wouldn't understand now, but you will," he says.

At this point, I think we're done, and I can get back to my work. But Solomon continues. "Pastor, God said to tell you one more thing. God said you can't take this church to a new dimension until you let go of the weight in your heart."

Now he has my attention, and as he continues to talk, I realize he's describing matters of my heart that only God would know about. Not some moral failure or scandal, but deep things that have gone wrong in my heart. It dawns on me that the weight of climbing up levels has just about killed me. For the first time in my life, I begin to sense the possibility of a new way to just *be* in the kingdom.

By now I'm listening with my whole heart. When he's done, the car-wash boy says good-bye and leaves.

Thinking back on that encounter, Clint told me, "By the way, the question of levels versus dimension has been a defining one for our community over the years. We're still amazed at what we are discovering."

Do you see what a breakthrough this issue can represent for any Christ follower? We're so inclined to try to make things happen for God. Every week we're tempted to get out a measuring stick. Did we get higher? Are we sliding down? And we figure that God is measuring too.

But God isn't measuring anything. He only wants us to live in a dimension that is already there. Week after week, He is simply inviting us to be part of what He is *already* doing. Somehow the car-wash boy—who will probably never get higher on any human level and isn't trying—got the kingdom.

The kid is already in it.

For both Clint and me, the message from the car-wash boy started us on a new journey of faith that has been freeing and scary at times too. Living out of control does that to you. It has brought me back to a key verse in Colossians that says Jesus has rescued us out of the kingdom of darkness and transferred us into the kingdom of the Son. We've been taken from one dimension and moved to another. No levels, just transferred by the King.

Choosing to live in the kingdom dimension creates some major shifts in our thinking. One of those is the shift from advancing to embracing. I don't see my life now as one in which I advance the kingdom of God. It is advancing all by itself.

Jesus explained it this way: His kingdom is like a tiny mustard seed. God Himself has planted it in the field of our world.

> Though it is the smallest of all your seeds, yet when it grows, it is the largest of garden plants and becomes a tree, so that the birds of the air come and perch in its branches.

The seed of the kingdom is growing and spreading organically into a mighty dimension that will one day be the home of all living things. Even now, the kingdom dimension, like the life in that mustard seed, is absolutely real, and it doesn't need my effort to make it so. Yet since the kingdom starts so small and grows so utterly unnoticed, you and I can miss it when it's right in front of us.

Jesus explained it another way:

> The kingdom of heaven is like yeast that a woman took and mixed into a large amount of flour until it worked all through the dough.

Do you see the revolutionary kingdom in this one-sentence picture? Invisibly, silently, seemingly without power, seemingly absent, the presence of the kingdom is spreading through the flour until the flour becomes bread. But the miracle of the yeast is God's work, not yours or mine.

The kingdom is a dimension I acknowledge, I live in, I participate in. Yet it's never a level I achieve. It is a lot less like building the business of Christianity and a lot more like slipping into the matrix of Jesus.

In leaving the levels, I am called by Jesus to embrace His way of being in the world. That means that church is not about getting big but about creating space where we live out the new kingdom humanity as He taught it. It's sad to see pastors who are burned out because they can't get off the treadmill or believers who are ready to chuck their faith in Jesus because they are tired of trying to perform.

Following Jesus isn't about us; it's about Him. I can't embrace the kingdom when my arms are full of me. So I have to let go. Then Jesus can give me a new way of being.

At first we see it only in glimpses: a kind gesture, giving to others in need, saying no to personal gain because it may cost us our souls, pursuing relationships with people whom Jesus wants us to love.

Embracing is hard, but it's also freeing.

I don't know what you have to let go of. I know I have to let go of things all the time. What I am realizing a few years after leaving the levels behind is that our eyes begin to see differently. We notice the kingdom dimension of life, but only slowly. It's like when you walk from a completely darkened room into the blazing sunlight of noon. At first you squint and draw back. The whole world seems blurred by the sun's rays. But after a few seconds, you see normally. In fact, you see more clearly than you did in that dark room.

Seeing the kingdom may take a few seconds.

Another shift that Jesus invites us to make is from producing to growing. A producer puts parts together and makes something new happen. You produce a veggie lasagna from cheese, asparagus, tomato sauce, and pasta. Throw in some eggplant, if you like. You produce a BMW from auto parts. But everything you produce is already dead. It's just a thing. One day it will get old and rot or rust and waste away.

Compare a producer to a grower. A grower stands in his garden. He leans over growing things to tend them with water and fertilizer and loving care. He watches with pleasure and expectation as his plants accomplish the *one thing* he can't make happen: they grow.

The kingdom of Jesus is alive and growing, but not because we make it grow. We plant seeds of life. We water and weed. We sweat and hope and pray. But the dynamic of life in the garden is the kingdom at work. It is the life of God springing up around us.

In the kingdom, the places we put our hearts into and work at are places where we are collaborating with kingdom life. We don't collaborate with programs or buildings or technologies, although God can use those for important ends. Rather we notice and invite and affirm the kingdom in people.

In the nervous young mom next to us on the bus.

In the migrant farmworker waiting in line ahead of us at a 7-Eleven.

In the man next door who's duking it out with old age and chemotherapy.

In the child in our own household who's crossing the threshold from playground to pimple hell.

The kingdom *is*. We *are* witnesses.

Kingdom life is found when we articulate the good news of Jesus Christ to those who have not yet heard. Jesus is the doorway into the kingdom. But kingdom life thrives also in the beautiful ordinary, not just when we're doing ministry or working at a church.

If you're a writer, let God use your interests and abilities to grow His kingdom in you and through you. That doesn't require that you write only about Jesus or put a fish symbol on your manuscript. It means that you write as one who lives for and in another dimension.

If you're a businessperson, don't bow your knee to fame, money, or making a name for yourself. Instead, excel in your area of expertise so that people can see what good, true, and beautiful business looks like.

If you're a musician, architect, stay-at-home mother, or the guy with the burrito cart in Pioneer Courthouse Square, the kingdom of God is here and is inviting you to collaborate with what God is doing in your real world.

You have the necessary permission slip. You can let go of performing and achieving and striving. You can invite the life of God to rise up all around you. You can sing it into your everyday world.

Experience the seed.

Look for that mysterious yeast, invisibly spreading.

Voices

When My Brothers Were Too Young to Be Wise

When my brothers were too young to be wise
but too old to name things creatively,
they invented a game called:
Let's take turns jumping off Tom's roof
and throw the cat after the person who jumped.
    At least they took turns…

Later, when my brothers were too young to be wise
but old enough to put their scientific knowledge to use,
they played a game called:
Let's pour gas over this giant pile of weeds
and then light it on fire.
    At least the doctor said
    that their eyebrows will grow back…

Later, when my brother was old enough to be depressed
but too young to know how to cope,
he would play a game called:
Let's go to Tom's house and do a lot of drugs
and drink all his stepdad's beer.
    At least there was that one English teacher
    who asked if something was wrong…
    but what could you say?

We are so poorly equipped to deal with these
       troubles,
and there are so few doctors of the soul these
       days...
   What is there to do?
I know some people who fight it all their lives,
kicking against the goads till they bleed to death.
Others, like Dad, ignore it,
thinking that hard work, sunshine, and
the passing of time will resolve it.
Still others, like Mom, ostracize and cast blame
by leaving condemnatory evangelical polemics
       taped
to your bathroom mirror.

But now my brothers and I are old enough
to begin to be wise,
yet still young enough to climb the cold roof
to talk and to smoke.
So I will play a new game with you called:
Let's go together and bear one another's burdens.
   At least I will not laugh at your pain,
   I will not try to fix your problems,
   I will not ignore your suffering
   or condemn you with my piety...
I will simply lie here next to you in the cold
while we breathe our smoky prayers to God.

—Raeben Nolan

Jesus' Kingdom of Peace

> Glory to God in the highest,
> and on earth peace to men on whom
> his favor rests.

It was two weeks before Christmas in Portland. The rain had settled in for its nine- to ten-month stint, and a thick layer of clouds lay over the city. This didn't stop Portlanders from going about their daily business. In fact, we continued to bike to work, jog, hike, and shop. No local would be caught dead with an umbrella. That's how we know who the tourists are.

I was driving home from the office with my daughter, who had been volunteering at the church. I turned on NPR as the windshield wipers squeaked back and forth in the pouring rain. The news was reporting a shooting at a mall. Our conversation went silent. Of course I assumed this was happening somewhere else. Tragedies like this always seem to happen somewhere else. Then the reporter announced that the shooting took place at Clackamas Town Center, just a few miles from where we live.

I immediately called my wife. Then breathed a sigh of relief—each of my family members was home and safe. But others were not.

The lone gunman, wearing a hockey mask and carrying a semiautomatic machine gun, had dashed into the mall just past the food court and begun spraying bullets. Two people were killed; a teenager was taken in critical condition to Oregon Health and Science University Hospital.

The city and the nation were in shock. The mall was on lockdown for hours. Over the next few days, I heard story after story of people who were there, people who knew the victims. Every story was laced with fear and imaginings of what could have happened and horror at what did happen. But there was still more horror to come.

Three days later, a gunman in Newtown, Connecticut, stormed into an elementary school and killed twenty-six people. Most of the victims were first graders. The town reeled from the massacre, and the rest of the country reeled and grieved with them.

In both tragedies, as the media tried to piece together the facts, we were all trying to tell a story that made sense. We wanted it to make sense. We longed for it to make sense. We *needed* it to make sense. But when children are senselessly murdered and holiday shoppers are fleeing for their lives, no sense can be found in such stories. Life feels suddenly fragile and all the more precious. Evil seems to win the day, and unwanted memories are burned into our consciousness.

My daughter and I will never forget that drive home.

A few weeks later, we held our Christmas services at Imago. We were to celebrate this incredible announcement that God has given us His Son. That our King has arrived. That He changes everything. The angels announce, "Joy to the world, and on earth peace to men on whom His favor rests."

But does Jesus and His kingdom really make a difference in moments like these in Portland and Newtown? Does Jesus truly bring peace to the world?

Questions fill our minds every time tragedy strikes. Is God good? Why did He allow this? Where is the kingdom now? If we are going to take kingdom living seriously, we can't live in denial of the pain and questions life brings. We can't be bold followers of Jesus and ambassadors of His kingdom if, in the back of our minds, we think that we are unsafe under His reign, that in the end He may not be a good King.

So where is the peace? How do we come to grips with the reality that our world presents? How do we live in that reality while experiencing the peace that supposedly is given to us in Christ and His kingdom?

First of all, what is peace? What do we mean when we say that word? What is the peace Jesus talked about, the peace that is ascribed to Him?

Biblically, the Hebrew word for "peace" is *shalom,* which is a sense of harmony in all relationships. It's harmony with God and His creation, with one another, with the earth. It's the dream of all things working in a rhythm of sorts, of everything being the way it's supposed to be.

Harmony in music means that the instruments, the musicians, and the conductor are all working together, all playing the same composition. When we look through the lens of music, we understand harmony as well as its opposite: disharmony.

If you are a parent with kids in fifth or sixth grade, you may have attended an elementary school band concert. Few people buy tickets to such an event, but for the people who attend, it's amazing. You're watching your kid, and she's playing her instrument. It might be a tuba or a flute, but she is playing with all her might. As a parent, you are proud of her, and though it sounds rough, it's a beautiful roughness.

When I was in fourth grade, I played trumpet until the band teacher asked me not to. I thought I was ripping it up, but it turns out I wasn't. The reason for my self-confidence? My mom, my grandmother, and my great-grandmother kept telling me I was great! The truth, though, was I was awful, and the band teacher fired me, at nine years old, from the trumpet. Next, I took up what the teacher called percussion, but I knew a triangle when I saw one.

Let's say you are listening to an elementary school symphony and your child has a solo. How nervous are you? Let's just say when she hits a wrong note, you can feel it in your gut. It makes you and everyone else cringe. That's disharmony.

No one has to ask, "Did you hear that really awful noise in the middle of the song? Was that supposed to be there?" Everyone knows it was jarring, that it didn't belong. The feeling you have when a note goes bad? That isn't peace. That's the opposite of peace.

When we look out at the world, we hear those off notes. Sometimes we feel them deeply. That December week, the brutal discord of the shootings was heard around the world. We watched the news, and everyone knew, *That's not the way it's supposed to be.* We shuddered and wept. Where is the peace?

If we are honest, all of us play broken songs. No matter how hard we try, we still add to the discord and disharmony in this epic musical. We know from our own stories that this is not the way it's supposed to be.

So how does Jesus bring peace? How does He bring *shalom*? How does He bring these chords together? Picture God as a triune master conductor. He's Father, Son, and Spirit, and He creates everything that has life and being in it. Everything is created to live in freedom. Each piece of creation gets to make its own sound, whether it's a clanking noise or a lilting melody.

In His infinite wisdom, this God takes all these sounds and brings them into the fullness of His purposes. He creates a heavenly symphony with the beauty and love of Christ. When we hear, see, or feel the off notes, the truth is that they are real, and you and I have played some of them. But when God hears them, He doesn't cringe and say, "They've ruined My symphony!" Instead, He includes the bad notes in His concert. In His infinite creativity, He adds another theme, another layer, and somehow our noise is brought into a new composition.

Think of the off notes you have hammered out over the years or even this week. They might not be as ear shattering as a heinous shooting spree, but all the off notes are treated the same way by the Master Conductor.

God takes each of the dark noises blared into our lives, wreaking havoc, and He weaves them into a massive, grand, multifaceted song that has so many layers and themes that only heaven has the ears to hear it all. Those layers are filled with redemption, so that all the things in us and in our world, even those that resist His perfect rhythm, are grafted into the song in a way that fulfills His ultimate purposes.

He uses even broken notes to make His song beautiful, to make His beautiful song ours.

Let's look at this another way. J. R. R. Tolkien is best known for *The Hobbit* and *The Lord of the Rings,* but he wrote another story that takes place even before those books. It's called *The Silmarillion.* Within the first few pages, Tolkien expresses his vision of God as a conductor with an enemy trying to ruin his composition.

Ilúvatar represents the triune God conductor character, while Melkor, the archangel of music, corresponds to the person of Satan. As Ilúvatar creates his symphony, Tolkien tells us that it seems good to him, but "it came into the heart of Melkor to interweave matters of his own imagining that were not in accord with the throne of Ilúvatar; for he sought therein to increase the power and glory of the part assigned to himself."

In the freedom of his being and in the exercise of his gifts, Melkor proceeds to create dissonant chords against the direction of Ilúvatar. In doing this, he creates disharmony. He seeks to destroy peace.

Then the discord of Melkor spread ever wider, and melodies which had been heard before foundered in a sea of turbulent sound. But Ilúvatar sat and hearkened until it seemed that about his throne there was a raging storm, as of dark waters that made war one upon another in an endless wrath that would not be assuaged.

There is an enemy, Jesus said in His parables and teaching. Like Melkor, he comes to disrupt *shalom*. He comes to create a turbulent sea within our hearts and our world. We too easily dance to his beats and then blame the Conductor for our misuse of freedom and the noise that results from our misuse. So how does our God deal with the painful and often violent notes that His enemy creates and His creatures play along to?

Then Ilúvatar arose, and the Ainur [Melkor's tribe] perceived that he smiled; and he lifted up his left hand and a new theme began amid the storm, like and yet unlike to the former theme, and it gathered power and had new beauty.

Did you hear that? Ilúvatar smiled! What was Tolkien thinking? Was he out of his mind? No, I think he was on to something that is true and biblical.

This is the Conductor who causes all things to work "for the good of those who love him, who have been called according his purpose." This is the God of Joseph, who lived through the violent discord of being sold by his own brothers into slavery but could ultimately proclaim to them, "You intended to harm me, but God intended it for good." This is the almighty Conductor who continues to weave good into the evil doings of Melkor, you, me, and even into the evil doings of disturbed shooters who enter classrooms and extinguish twenty children's lives.

In Tolkien's story, Melkor continues to create more and more discord against the melodies of Ilúvatar. His attempts grow increasingly violent, and Ilúvatar must raise his right hand and create yet another theme that grows amid the confusion.

> And it seemed at last that there were two musics progressing at one time before the seat of Ilúvatar, and they were utterly at variance. The one was deep and wide and beautiful, but slow and blended with an immeasurable sorrow, from which its beauty chiefly came.

Finally after many attempts by Melkor to contradict Ilúvatar's beauty, the music stops and Ilúvatar rises and speaks.

> Mighty are the Ainur, and mightiest among them is Melkor; but that he may know, and all the Ainur, that I am Ilúvatar, those things that ye have sung, I will show them forth, that ye may see what ye have done. And thou, Melkor, shalt see that no theme may be played that hath not its uttermost source in me, nor can any alter the music in my despite. For he that attempteth this shall prove but mine instrument in the devising of things more wonderful, which he himself hath not imagined.

I love the picture Tolkien paints. God says, "No theme can be played that doesn't have its source in Me." That does not mean God does evil; it means all things that humans do or create are limited. God is the King, and we cannot escape or usurp Him. So everything we do, be it worship or evil, we create within the boundaries of our limits.

Here is the beauty that brings peace. Because God is limitless in His being and in His love, it means that evil and death have a limit. Sin has a limit, but God's purposes do not. He can create theme after theme in the midst of creation's rebellion, and He will triumph in love as He incorporates our pain and our rebellion into His symphony.

This brings a kingdom of peace into the dark harmonies of our world. Because God is good, He creates us in freedom and He weaves our abuse of our freedom into His goodness, love, and beauty. God is reconciling all things to himself through Christ. He's taking our broken song and redeeming it. He's conducting His symphony and making beauty with our mess. No act of evil can overcome the direction in which He's taking the song.

So now we can see more clearly how Jesus is the Prince of Peace in His kingdom of peace. Jesus steps into our humanity. As He does, He plays life as it's supposed to be played, in perfect step with the Father, keeping perfect time in the rhythm of the Spirit. As He breaks into our world, we see Him bringing harmony and *shalom* into a world that's broken.

He is filled with compassion. He takes rebellion against Himself and creates something new called *grace* and *mercy.* He overpowers dissonant notes. As Jesus, He lived His life in perfect time until He was captured by the forces of evil and nailed to a cross. Melkor smiled. This perfect, innocent man died under the power of death.

The stage went dark for three days. No instruments were played. It seemed as though that dark, pounding minor chord of death had triumphed. The people wept, disciples ran, hope fled, and peace was a lost love. For three days, no faith, no hope, no peace.

Then it happened. As if the Father stood and raised both hands at dawn on the third day, the strings softly broke in. Timpani added a thunderous cadence, rolling in the distance but racing closer.

The stone was rolled away. Christ walked out of the grave. He had conquered death! The angel choir broke into a "Hallelujah!" chorus. This powerful crescendo built to a roar, and our God swallowed up sin and death once and for all!

Out of the darkest chord that had ever been played, He created the most beautiful theme in His symphony. He took the shrill death of the Son of God and turned it into a sacrament of salvation. Communion is perhaps the greatest picture of His infinite wisdom at work in our redemption. Every time we take it, we find a very present peace in the midst of our broken song.

His resurrection symphony did not stop there, though. A few days later, flutes and woodwinds broke in, and Jesus sent His Spirit to rest upon His people, empowering them to sing *His* song, to play in *His* symphony of *shalom.*

That's why He can enable us to live in the way we're meant to live, in union with this master conductor who is Father, Son, and Spirit.

I understand that some people will think this sounds like fantasy. But I believe it's the most epic story that has ever been told, and it *is* an absolute reality.

Whatever dark, broken chord you think permeates your life, God's love triumphs. Our triune master conductor is orchestrating your broken song into the amazing masterpiece of His song. Think through all the disharmony that the Melkors of this world have tried to inflict. God is not ignorant of any of it, nor is He the author of sin and death. Rather, when each evil chord is played, He raises his hand—and smiles.

He picks up His baton. There's a hush as He stands, and then taps His baton on the music stand.

Tap, tap, tap.

He takes count of our broken notes.

- Where there's a dark chord of sin, He plays forgiveness.
- Where there's abuse, He brings healing.
- Where there's violence, He brings peace.
- Where there's grief, He brings comfort.
- Where there's suffering, He brings wholeness.
- Where there's betrayal, He brings faithfulness.
- Where there's abandonment, He is the eternal Father.
- Where there's addiction, He brings freedom.
- Where there's greed, He brings generosity.
- Where there's chaos, He brings peace.

In the end, He will sing over us the words of John's Revelation: "There will be no more death or mourning or crying or pain, for the old order of things has passed away.... I am making everything new!"

So to you, wherever you are and whatever notes you are playing today, I say with triumphant certainty: *Shalom!* The kingdom is among us today.

Already, Not Yet

> Jesus told them another parable: "The kingdom of heaven is like a man who sowed good seed in his field. But while everyone was sleeping, his enemy came and sowed weeds among the wheat, and went away. When the wheat sprouted and formed heads, then the weeds also appeared."

While everyone slept, an enemy came… Do you feel the sadness, the disappointment, the bitter frustration in those words? Instinctively, we sense the historic truth in the story Jesus told about the enemy who sowed weeds among the wheat. We see the awful evidence all around us. No matter how hard we try, a corrupting influence sneaks into our families, a destroyer invades our bodies, a culture of hatred attacks our cities, famine and poverty lurk about. No sooner have we repented—so we can see the kingdom and quit the levels and experience it—than we collide with the "real world." We live on a planet where organized religion, greedy corporations, sudden cancer, and dark spiritual forces (to name a few opposing forces) compete with God for the same turf.

We feel this competition deeply. Take new life in Christ. Jesus is bringing His goodness and beauty in and through us. He's showing His face among the poor, in the joy of a baby's cooing. Yet there is Christless sickness, starvation, and death everywhere. All are true.

My word for these competing realities about life in the kingdom is *tension*. Tension helps me to understand a kingdom that is already here and also not yet here. Both are true.

If I hold on to one set of observations but not the other, I might feel less at odds with what I see happening around me, but I will be living in make-believe. Consider two examples of what goes wrong when followers of Jesus let go of the both/and truth of tension.

On the one hand, I see some evangelical communities and traditions that camp on the not-yet end of the truth of the kingdom. They tend to look away from the disadvantaged, from issues of injustice or raping of the natural world for profit because—they're relieved to tell you—"Jesus is coming soon." They're happily "in" (sinners are "out"). They're mostly just putting in time at the Jesus station, waiting for the salvation train to arrive and take them home. Why should they look for or participate in a kingdom that is wholly not yet?

On the already-here end of the spectrum, some Christians seem to expect themselves and others who sincerely follow Jesus to enjoy a charmed life. Their only obligation in the kingdom is strict personal piety. They're clinging to an already-only ideal, but it inevitably leads to narrowness and disillusionment.

Healthy tension comes when we choose to embrace the paradoxical truths of already *and* not yet (for more on this tension, see appendix 1). It's a step of maturity, and it's part of living in the kingdom of Jesus. We embrace a kingdom that is breaking in but finding itself in opposition with much of what is already here. It is a kingdom in conflict.

The teachings of Jesus on His kingdom in Matthew 13 address this paradox from different angles. Each parable shows how the kingdom is already beautifully present in our flawed world and how Jesus invites us as His flawed people to respond.

"A farmer went out to sow his seed," Jesus told His listeners (it was another day by the lake). And then He unfolded a simple story of a man, soil, and seeds.

A hardworking farmer walks out to his field on a spring day. At his side he carries a full bag of seed. With one hand, he holds open the bag; with the other, he grabs handfuls of seed and scatters them in wide arcs from side to side. Will this planting lead to a plentiful harvest come fall or to something less?

Jesus described how, as the seed scatters, it falls on different kinds of ground. In some places, it falls on the path, where birds quickly gobble it up. In others, the seed falls among rocks, where it sprouts quickly. But since the seed can't take root, it soon dies. In other places, the seed falls among weeds and thorns, where it doesn't last long either. But some seed falls onto fertile, deep soil. And there it grows. Come fall, each seed that fell in the good soil bears abundantly. In fact, the heads of grain bear up to a hundred new seeds in return for each seed that went into the ground.

The soil in His parable, Jesus explains, stands for different types of welcome and responsiveness in the hearers of His message. Some don't understand. Some do but don't act on what they've heard. Some fall away once worldly distractions or hard times come. In these three kinds of people, the truth of the kingdom produces little or nothing. But some receive the message like deep, fertile soil. These hearers receive, understand, and reproduce the kingdom seed many times over.

Pay attention, Jesus says, because in a mysterious but powerful way, the condition of your heart radically dictates what the kingdom is going to look like in your life. If you wrap all your hopes and dreams around it and let it sink far into your inner being, the kingdom of Jesus will live in you and bear fruit.

What kind of heart do you have? What kind of soil do you see in your faith community?

In dozens of ways at Imago Dei, we come together to receive the seeds of the kingdom. "Fall here," we tell the sower. "Fall deep." Each kernel is bursting with promise, with life, with incredible potential. But the human soil of each heart where the seed lands is different, and that difference radically alters outcomes.

For some, week after week, the birds win. The truth is gone from their awareness within minutes, I'd guess. Gone by the time, say, they've walked out the doors and turned the corner onto Ankeny Street. Other influences they serve have already come along and ripped the seeds of the kingdom out of their hearts.

Other people hear the good news of the kingdom and immediately feel highly motivated. But there's no follow-through. What are they actually willing to change to help that seed grow? As it turns out, there's not much.

Others genuinely receive the seed of truth, but over time the worries and obsessions of life choke out the amazing harvest they want and could have had. If you've hung around a community of Christ followers for very long, you know exactly what I'm saying. Work, school, relationships, family—a lot of what's good in life can squeeze out what's eternal and what's best. Plenty of truth goes in week after week, but unfortunately not much growth or fruitfulness ever comes out.

There are, however, those who receive the kingdom desperately and expectantly—like oxygen, like food for starving people, like hope going down into their deepest beings. They value and protect and act on it. Pretty soon a harvest of kingdom living starts showing up all over the place—in how they think, in what they care about, in what they do with their time and who they spend it with. Of course, the world out there on Ankeny is just as distracting for them. The web of requirements they live in is just as demanding and conflicting. But they've embraced the kingdom of Jesus now. And in all the mess and noise and tension of their lives, God's agenda is showing up.

And it's beautiful.

Beauty in tension.

How does the already—not yet dynamic of the kingdom manifest itself in the ordinary dirt of family?

My son Josh is the oldest of my four kids, but only by twenty minutes. His sister Kaylee showed up right behind him. One hot summer day when he was thirteen, he came down with a fever, and his hip was hurting. On my way out the door that day, Jeanne told me she would be taking him to the pediatric clinic.

Later, I was drinking coffee at the Urban Grind with my friend Stacy, who was just back from a year in Venezuela, where he had been working with college students. Stacy was telling me about the amazing people he had met and the great conversations he'd had with people about Jesus and how people were coming to know Jesus personally and following Him in His way of being in the world. Everywhere he looked, the kingdom was breaking in. It was one of those conversations you cherish, sitting with an old friend and catching up on the story of God in this world.

We were only about ten minutes into our conversation when my cell rang. It was Jeanne, and she was still at the clinic.

"They don't know what's wrong with Josh," she said.

The doctors were very concerned. They were doing an MRI and blood work. Jeanne sounded worried, and my heart sank. Stacy knew I had to go. As we parted, he prayed for Josh and our whole family.

It was a tough day. One medical test after another and no solid answers. By evening, we were checking Josh into the children's unit at Emanuel Hospital and meeting with an infectious disease specialist.

Tension.

Tension filled my heart and soul and spirit at that moment and for the next several days.

Finally Josh was diagnosed with a staph infection in his sacroiliac joint. The specialist had encountered his condition only three times in her career.

At first the antibiotics didn't seem to help. Josh's fever spiked over and over. It was a depressing and scary time. Nothing is worse than watching your child suffer. Days passed. We saw other kids checking into the hospital and a day or so later checking out. But Josh was not getting better. Jeanne and I took shifts at his bedside.

On the third day, they started Josh on his second antibiotic. We spent every possible minute together in that room. Laughing, making jokes, praying, worrying, asking nurses the same questions over and over, trying desperately to get some comfort. Still it was a time when our hearts connected powerfully with our son—we in our helplessness, he in his pain, and a love between us that is more than words can tell.

Sometimes I walked the hospital halls. I saw beautiful bald three-year-old girls who were battling leukemia. I met a nineteen-year-old Hispanic boy named Alex who'd been hit by an SUV. I saw beauty and suffering everywhere. Tension. If you hang out in children's hospitals, you can't escape it. In every room, on every parent's face, you can tell that life is not the way it is supposed to be. A crazy kind of empathy and community develops. You're filled with compassion for every dad and mom you see. You know, without a word, exactly what they're feeling.

But it's a messy compassion. Every time a kid leaves and yours isn't getting any better, you feel a wave of anger and envy and impatience—

like you've been waiting in line to be rescued, but when the rescuers come, it's not for you.

Sitting in a hospital, you're faced with the strong reality of the not yet. In heaven there will be no hospitals, no doctors, no nurses, no bald toddlers with cancer, no parents whose eyes are full of confusion and pain and mourning. No tears. All misery will be gone. But it isn't gone yet.

Weeks passed. People around Portland and around the world prayed for Josh. I prayed a lot too, and almost all my prayers were filled with tension. *God, did You put this infection in my son's back to teach me and him something? God, did You have the SUV hit Alex so he would learn something? What does this mean? What is it for?*

I didn't get many answers, but something was growing inside me. I began to accept, on a very personal level, that although the kingdom of God is already here, it's also not yet.

During those weeks, some well-meaning people gave us the right answers. "God knows what's happening," they said. "Josh will be fine because we're praying." The right answers seem right to say, of course, and they seem right when you hear them, but they don't help much. To be honest, the right answers began to make us angry. Somehow Christians have a hard time saying things like, "I don't know why the hell this is happening or how this will end. You guys must be scared to death." I guess we all need to be able to explain life down to every last detail, even when the answers don't mean anything to us. We just can't stand the questions. But in the kingdom of God, I have come to believe, it is all right not to have all the answers, and I think Jesus likes it even more when we don't make up answers that are safe and easy but hollow.

Just because people prayed did not mean that Josh would be okay.

Just because God knew what was happening didn't mean I did. Or that I knew how God would intervene for our family.

Just because I knew a Bible verse that says God will answer when I pray didn't mean I wouldn't lose my kid to some stupid killer infection. His answers are not always my answers.

It's exactly this type of shallow religion that makes people afraid to walk through the wild and untamed fields of the kingdom of God.

Ever notice? Some people seem to have a Gap version of Christianity: a polished franchise faith where everyone is always winsome and smiling. But I'm not interested. During those days when Josh couldn't leave the hospital, I was constantly aware that my son could die and that, if he did, I'd never be able to replace him. I believe I was *supposed* to be aware of that.

My friends Jim and Marilyn lost a son in Iraq. I thought a lot about them during those days in the children's ward. No matter how hard I tried, I couldn't come up with a good answer for their pain. For several years, I've seen the grief written into their lives. I've seen the courage it takes for them just to come to church.

Tension hurts.

"Our Father in heaven," we plead. "Your kingdom come. Please."

I wonder if Jesus was thinking of lost sons and daughters when He told His next parable that day.

> The kingdom of heaven is like a man who sowed good seed in his field. But while everyone was sleeping, his enemy came and sowed weeds among the wheat, and went away. When the wheat sprouted and formed heads, then the weeds also appeared.
>
> The owner's servants came to him and said, "Sir, didn't you sow good seed in your field? Where then did the weeds come from?"
>
> "An enemy did this," he replied.

The servants asked him, "Do you want us to go and pull them up?"

"No," he answered, "because while you are pulling the weeds, you may root up the wheat with them. Let both grow together until the harvest. At that time I will tell the harvesters: First collect the weeds and tie them in bundles to be burned; then gather the wheat and bring it into my barn."

In this story, Jesus paints a picture of the already–not yet reality of His kingdom. I don't like the picture—especially the "enemy came" part, followed by the "let both grow together until the harvest" part.

Jesus told His disciples that day that He is the sower, the field is the world, "the good seed stands for the sons of the kingdom," and the one who sows the weeds is the devil. Jesus promises that "at the end of the age…everything that causes sin and all who do evil" will be uprooted and thrown into the fire. "My day of judgment *will* come," Jesus is saying. No more weeds after that, just wheat. After that, "the righteous will shine like the sun in the kingdom of their Father."

But for now, let the weeds grow. Let the wheat of your young sons grow together with the weeds of scary infections and hate bombs.

I remember when my friend Scott was killed. I went to the grave site with his family to lead the memorial. The whole time there in the cemetery we felt the sting of death. The awful mess of grief and rage and unfairness was right there under our feet. I hated it.

But no one dies in the kingdom of God. It is in the kingdom of Satan, our enemy, where death reigns. A pastor friend told me that as he was preparing for a funeral once, he decided to go through the Gospels to see how Jesus dealt with funerals. What he discovered was that Jesus did not much care for them. Every one He went to, He raised the person from the dead. Jesus doesn't do funerals, not even His own.

You have a friend who's dying of cancer. Everything in you wants that made right. You have a marriage that's falling apart. In your mind, that's neither fair nor right. A friend is murdered. Everything in you cries out, "This isn't right! God, where are You?"

At those times we must wait in faith and sorrow and hope for the end of not yet. The same Jesus who doesn't do funerals says to you, "Trust Me. My father is still at work in the world, still growing wheat, even turning weeds back into wheat. Look at the story of your life. But I am coming, and I'm coming with judgment. I'm going to make everything right."

I was standing in the parking lot of Emanuel Hospital on a hot August day, wishing I had a cigarette. My guts were twisted in the tension of the already here–not yet here kingdom. My family was living through the battle of it. Right there, in the shade of a tree in the parking lot, I realized the power in the truth of tension.

I don't think I'd seen it before. In the past, getting clobbered by the mess would've rocked my faith. I would have misunderstood what was going on and ended up believing that God was the One who was making my kid sick. It's very challenging to worship a God who knocks you down and then helps you back up. But in this new moment of tension and living in the reality of the kingdom, I experienced a clarity that I can only hope you find as well, because I know that the tension in your life is no different than mine, and it brings with it a faith-shattering punch if you miss this.

The kingdom of God is the kingdom of life, health, beauty, salvation, and freedom (to name just a few of its qualities). The enemy of the kingdom, whom the Bible refers to as Satan, is always attacking that life, that health, that beauty. He attacks spiritual freedom. He wants us to be paralyzed. His relentless attacks are why things are not the way they are supposed to be—yet.

But in the midst of all the tensions of life, the kingdom of God comes crashing in. It usually crashes in quietly, though. God showed up all through our situation with Josh:

- Nurses were kind.
- Josh and I shared gut-busting laughter in the hospital room.
- A friend arranged for the guitarist from one of Josh's favorite bands to come to the hospital. (That was really cool!)
- People prayed and watched our kids and loved us. People sat with us, cried with us, laughed with us.

In those moments, the tension receded. It had to wait while the love of God filled the room and flooded our hearts. The kingdom of darkness and ugliness, for those hours, was pushed outside the door by grace.

I realized that God didn't create or send Josh's sickness. He was not distant or unaware of it either. God's kingdom is present and real. He knows if a sparrow falls to the ground, Jesus said. But that doesn't mean God flicked the sparrow off the tree. Rather, He is present and aware and caring, even in the tension of death and sickness. In its own ways, Jesus' kingdom breaks in.

In our case, healing came. Josh got better. We were, and are, so grateful and relieved. For other children in that hospital, however, illnesses lingered or death came. We had to face it and release ourselves to that possibility for Josh too. If Josh had died—like Jim and Marilyn's son had died—our lives would never have been the same. Their lives won't be. I know beyond a shadow of a doubt that I would walk with a limp in my soul for the rest of my life. But the kingdom would be there in its beauty too—around and inside and ahead of that limping man.

God has this amazing judo move that He uses to attack the kingdom of darkness. He causes all things to work for good to those who love Him, the Bible says. God takes what is meant for evil and turns it for good, if we trust Him at those times and embrace His sovereign goodness even in the midst of our pain and loss. The good He works for us will be a fore-taste of the ultimate restoration that will occur when His kingdom comes in all its fullness. It doesn't make the cost of death less real. But it shows a way through. I think of the song "Tension (Is a Passing Note)" from Sixpence None the Richer, which declares that we can embrace tension as a brief note in a broader chord of beauty.

I felt that in the hospital parking lot. I didn't know yet what would happen to Josh, but in the stillness I heard the passing note of love. I knew that somehow the kingdom of God would still prevail with goodness and healing. The passing note our family heard was from the "already" king-dom, and it was absolutely true.

Meanwhile, in this season of tension and mess, we wait for the King to come in His full glory and to express His final authority over life and death and evil. We wait for His kingdom to bring complete beauty and to put an end to "not yet" forever.

One day, the passing note will swell into a beautiful, beautiful chord that will never end.

PART 3

Practicing the Presence of the Kingdom

When I compared the vision for life in the kingdom that Jesus put forth in the Gospels with the experience I had at church as a new Christian, I noticed a discrepancy. Jesus' fresh perspectives on money, suffering, justice, and love had been refashioned into a tidy way of life for those who did their best to convey that they no longer needed much of what He had to say. At eighteen, I sensed the problem without quite being able to say it. In all the tidiness, the wonder of the gospel of Jesus seemed to be disappearing. As a recent convert, I was alive in that wonder. It was changing my life. But looking around, I realized that most of Jesus' followers lived pretty much like everyone else—except we hoped for heaven. The Christian life began to look like one long waiting game of Bible studies and boring parties. If I was lucky, a bus would hit me and I'd go straight to heaven. Until then, the kingdom life I was reading about in the Gospels would have to wait. I felt disappointed—like I had entered C. S. Lewis's wardrobe, full of anticipation, but instead of standing in a magical place with fawns and witches and every kind of possibility, I had somehow managed to walk through the wardrobe and into a dentist's office. People sat around reading magazines and asking me to calm down, to be quiet, to take a seat. They said it very nicely, of course, like you would in a dentist's office. The place was clean, with polite smiles everywhere, sterile smells, and bad Muzak. What are you supposed to do in a waiting room except try to kill the time? I did a lot of that. I killed time in college groups. In church. In Bible college. I even killed time as a pastor.

But leaning back in my chair one day, I realized that the walls of the waiting room were actually as thin as paper. Behind the veil of Western evangelicalism existed an untamed, revolutionary reality. The world on the other side of the wardrobe did exist, I realized. You just have to tear down the fake walls first, kill the fake music, and let yourself go crashing with newborn, wide-eyed anticipation out into the world.

And there it is all around you. The kingdom of God.

Part 3 of *This Beautiful Mess* is my small attempt to begin to tear down the fake walls of a sterile kingdom. My hope for this section is that it will help begin important paradigm shifts in how we think about life. That we will begin to see the kingdom of God in ordinary miracles all around us. Because they're there, happening right now as you breathe, think, read, and focus on these words. What would happen if we recaptured appropriate wonder at the present reality of the kingdom? What if we could see it and could collaborate with the Spirit as it breaks into our world? What if we discovered the simple miracle of participating with God in His kingdom and practicing the presence of it all around us?

Practicing the presence of the kingdom changes how we see the world, our neighbors, and ourselves. It changes the way we use money, understand children, and play in creation. It causes us to stop and listen, see, touch, taste, and feel. The kingdom is found in justice breaking in all around us, in beauty in the midst of mess.

The kingdom calls us to be signposts along the road of life, pointing to the reality of heaven and our King. It calls us to hold that sign up among those who suffer. The kingdom shows up, and we stand in the midst of suffering with people who are suffering and declare to them that they are loved.

We are to be that kind of signpost, showing up all over the place.

8

Signposts of Heaven

You are the light of the world. A city on a hill cannot be hidden. Neither do people light a lamp and put it under a bowl. Instead they put it on its stand, and it gives light to everyone in the house. In the same way, let your light shine before men, that they may see your good deeds and praise your Father in heaven.

As you go, preach this message: "The kingdom of heaven is near." Heal the sick, raise the dead, cleanse those who have leprosy, drive out demons. Freely you have received, freely give.

After Jesus went back to heaven, Dan and Lynn, friends of mine, decided to start showing what heaven's response to homelessness might look like. Every night during cold weather, they loaded their car with blankets and socks and roamed Portland, looking for people who were trying to sleep on the streets. If the street people didn't look warm, Dan and Lynn would pull out an armload of comfort and tuck them in. These days, they have mobilized a team of like-minded agents. They call themselves Blanket Coverage. They've gotten some media attention, but they still operate mostly off the grid and out of sight. They like it that way. "What we hope is that when homeless people wake up to find that they have a new blanket and new socks, they'll think about God taking care of them, not us."

After Jesus went back to heaven, Kindra and Heather, two college students, decided to adopt. What they actually had in mind was adopting a whole apartment building—particularly, a low-income complex. They wanted to show heaven's response to a specific group in a specific place. So they went on a prayer walk and asked God to show them the place He wanted them to adopt. He did. The place where they ended up turned out to be a rehab center for single moms.

Kindra and Heather walked in and asked, "What can we do to help around here?"

The answer at first was, "Who do you think you are, just walking in here?" The recovering addicts didn't trust these well-dressed college girls. So the girls began by just holding babies. Week after week, they showed up to help the moms and listen to their stories of grief. In the process, Kindra and Heather learned a few things about drug addiction. For example, when you're serving coffee to a recovering addict, you always dump in a lot of sugar. Through it all, their message to the residents never wavered: Even if you reject us, we'll come back. We're not better; we're just here.

Before long, the girls received permission to take a family out for the day—to the zoo, the park, Dairy Queen. Anything to feel normal. At

Christmas, Kindra and Heather asked Imago to help the moms buy presents for their kids.

A year passed before any mom from rehab came to church. Even later, when one of the moms was baptized, she told our church that it was the trike for her son that did it. "That's when I felt in my heart that you cared," she said.

Just before Jesus went back to heaven, He said:

> You are the light of the world.... Let your light shine before men,
> that they may see your good deeds and praise your Father in
> heaven.

What some theologians call a "philosophy of ministry," Jesus summed up in one word: *go*. All His followers, then, are sent ones. And going is not complicated. Jesus painted simple pictures to show what going would look like. For example:

- A sent one is light.
- A sent one is salt.

Then Jesus gave His sent ones the largest mandate possible:

> Go into all the world and preach the good news to all creation.

Clear, simple, sweeping, revolutionary. But in the brief time since Jesus went back to heaven, His invitation has morphed into something less. Much less. We've turned *go* and *spread* into complicated programs best left to missionaries and preachers. We've reduced "all the world" and "all creation" to just the folks who walk through the front door at church.

And we've shrunk the good news to a short list of words that will save a soul from hell.

Isn't there more?

That's what I want us to dream about in this chapter. I've titled it "Signposts of Heaven" because followers of Jesus are sent out to be signposts pointing to the reality of His eternal kingdom. People who are signposts are "sent ones" who go to show the world the truth about how God feels about them.

To be signposts of the kingdom, we have to think creatively. After all, most of the issues we deal with don't exist in heaven. No one is homeless there. No one in heaven is addicted, trapped in greed, a workaholic, or lonely. Sometimes heaven looks like a warm blanket on a cold sidewalk. Sometimes it looks like a college girl who keeps showing up to help you carry your baby and your sorrows. Paradoxically, signposts of the kingdom radiate the most beauty when they're planted in the middle of the most mess.

These sent ones are some of the most original, humble, creative revolutionaries I know. And they are some of the most ordinary people I know too. You see, they're not better. They're just here.

To go on mission to all of creation is to express something indispensable about God's nature. In the Bible, the word *sent* occurs more than 650 times, and in a majority of its appearances, God is doing the sending. In the Old Testament, He sends angels to minister, manna to feed, and prophets to warn. He sends disasters to stop tyrants or discipline His people. He sends leaders to deliver. God is attentive to needs, and so He sends.

In the New Testament, the story of God reaches a climax as He sends His own Son into the world to suffer and die for our sin and to restore His creation. "I am the way and the truth and the life," Jesus says. "Anyone who has seen me has seen the Father." Jesus Christ is the ultimate signpost of heaven.

Nearing the end of His ministry on earth, Jesus turned to His followers and said, "As the Father has sent me, I am sending you." Then he sent the Holy Spirit to make our mission possible. In this story of God, we see the sequence of redemption: the Father sends the Son, the Son sends the Spirit, and the Father, Son, and Spirit send us, the church.

The idea of being sent isn't an agenda cooked up by some religious organization. It is the heartbeat of the living God. He is a God who sends and who goes Himself. In fact, without the word *sent*, you couldn't find the gospel in the Bible. That's why, when we go to people and places in need, we are expressing the Creator's nature. We are representing heaven and our King.

Of course, when God sends us, we don't have to go. Even the early apostles balked. For quite a while, they kept the good news in Jerusalem. I can understand why they didn't want to leave. People were responding to the gospel all over the place. A lot of lives were being changed. Why leave when the program was breaking all sorts of records? But God wanted them to go into all the world and to all creation with the good news. Perhaps to help get them going, He allowed persecution. Christians in Jerusalem started getting thrown in jail, beaten, even killed. Within just a few years, followers of Jesus had scattered throughout the Roman Empire, spreading the good news of the kingdom as they went.

I've noticed that most of us resist being sent. We're not used to being told where to go and what to do. But when we do go, we find that every culture has windows for redemption, places within a particular context where the gospel of Jesus speaks words of salvation, healing, and redemption. Those windows exist for you and me and your angry teenager and a depressed and lonely neighbor and the meth junkies among our rural poor and the cities of China and the stranger knocking at our door. Every town has places where heaven can show up, and the town will welcome it, because heaven's response is much better than the evil that is hurting those to whom we go. But every town has points of opposition too. When we stand up to be signposts and represent heaven, we can expect resistance. Nothing new about that, but when it's new to you, it can be pretty tough.

Going implies that we go somewhere new, to someone not like us, to some culture or subculture where we might not feel comfortable or knowledgeable or welcome. Certainly this means that sent ones need to become great students and listeners if we want to represent the kingdom well and for the long haul. We need to understand what it means to be relevant.

A lot of people say that the church isn't reaching America because it's not relevant. It's as if the church doesn't look sexy enough, but if we could just give it an extreme makeover, the culture around us would fall in love with it. "Man, look at the church!" they'd exclaim. "Church is looking *good*!" In no time, people would be camped outside like fans at a U2 concert, just waiting to nab the best seats.

Sounds ludicrous, doesn't it? But we do it. We try so hard to be cool. We say we need to have relevant music, relevant programs, relevant parking...

Of course, we're meant to communicate in an understandable way. I'm not saying we should try to be *irrelevant*. But relevance is a consequence of kingdom living, not a cause. We become relevant when we are committed to being that signpost of heaven in some part of our world. When we study Scripture, we find that relevance happens naturally when we choose to be real people caring for other real people. Even the real people who are not like us. Even the real people who don't hesitate to hate us.

Authentic relationships make us relevant.

When my friend Laura started volunteering at a local AIDS hospice, I remember how emotional the experience became for her at times. She decided that doing tasks around the hospice wasn't enough. She would love her patients and *keep on loving them* until they could feel it.

Since she's a musician, she'd play music for them. Over time, the people she met became her friends, not simply projects. When a patient died, she wept and mourned. The people at the hospice knew she loved them. She didn't have to work at being relevant because love given without any other agenda is always relevant. Relevance comes from relationship. It means we matter to someone, he or she matters to us, and we both know it.

Real relationship can keep us from being awkward and weird too. For example, if I'm having a conversation with somebody I just met and I say, "Now that we've enjoyed a cup of coffee, perhaps you'd like to hear my Christian testimony?" Awkward and weird like that. In a real relationship, we'd probably do a lot of listening first. We'd probably share our stories—all the ups and downs and struggles and dreams. In that context, our language and sensitivities would change. We'd get less churchy and strange. We'd get more authentic and interesting. We'd be more willing to risk knowing and being known.

The examples of Laura and others remind me that answering the call of Jesus to go actually requires so *little* of me. It's un-American, really. I don't need an organization in order to go with love. I don't need an Excel spreadsheet to know when relationship happens. Jesus said, "You are the light." I don't need a new wardrobe, a higher degree, a better vocabulary, a slimmer body, or a little more time before I can shine in the dark.

All I need is to say yes. Yes to being a signpost of the kingdom somewhere in my town with a particular people to whom God is sending me. Yes to following the example of the King by choosing to enter into broken worlds, not sit outside them with right answers. But I can go hopefully and boldly, in faith that this is God's agenda and I'm on mission from Christ. I can be a signpost of the kingdom because He has been one for me.

When I arrive wherever I am sent, I know what to do—I will love people until they can feel it, I will proclaim Jesus' reign with words and actions and love.

I remember the first time it dawned on me to love people in such a way that they know how God feels about them. One summer when I was working with students, I was invited to speak at a high school retreat on the Columbia River in central Washington State. Since I hadn't been invited to speak anywhere before, I thought this was clearly an act of God, so I grabbed my friend Jeff and we took off.

We arrived at the camp in blistering heat, with about fifty teenagers roaming around. Jeff and I found some shade and sat down to pray. As we were sitting there, praying about the session to come, I had a strong impression that God was telling me, "I want you to show these kids what I think about them." That sounded great, but honestly I had no idea what that meant. I figured I would try to communicate it when it was time to speak.

But it was the strangest thing. When I stood up to speak, all fifty campers seemed to be locked in a profound stupor. None of my jokes worked, none of my stories, nothing. From the football player to the shy girl in braces, they all just stared back at me. High schoolers can be intimidating when they look at you like that.

Why couldn't I communicate "Here is what God thinks about you"? I had been trained to speak and called by God to communicate His love to these kids. And there I stood, feeling like a fool.

Later, Jeff offered an opinion. "Yeah, I don't know what went wrong," he said. Very helpful.

So we just started hanging out with the campers. Jeff and I played football, got to know them one-on-one, interjected a little hope where we could, helped the big kid get up on water skis after the forty-second try. Mostly we were just present with them during the weekend, the whole time assuming that our reason for being there had not materialized and that nothing was happening.

It wasn't until the last night, when all fifty kids lined up to say good-bye to us, that Jeff and I realized that somewhere during the weekend, the window of redemption had opened. One by one they came to thank us for being friends, for listening, for playing. Most of them were crying, even the football player.

Jeff and I drove away humbled and in awe. We felt like the disciples must have felt when Jesus sent them out. A lot of times they didn't know where they were going or why or what they should do when they got there. They just went, and as it turned out, going was what mattered most.

At Imago, we're learners on this issue, but living as sent ones is shaping the DNA of who we are as Christ followers. We're finding that there are countless ways to plant signposts of the kingdom in the soil of our lives and our world. And we're intrigued by a kind of mysterious symmetry—a recognizable profile of God at work—that keeps surfacing as we go.

For example, we keep learning that *people come first*. Some look at Imago and notice a lot of ministries going out into the city. These are all simply pathways to people. Every person, no matter how battered by life, is created in the image of God. Their stories aren't just details that we have to push through so we can get them into the salvation chamber and out the other side in acceptable shape. Their journey itself is sacred. Our goal is to receive them as persons and in the process play a part in revealing God's heart to them.

Even feeding a hungry person isn't first about the food but about the person. Like some folks I know who decided to bless their neighborhood with a food distribution idea. They use a truck during the week to glean supplies at various grocery outlets, and then on weekends they set up a Saturday market in the parking lot of a low-income apartment complex. People walk through the aisles with shopping bags, thumping melons, picking out the food they want. It's all free. Why not just leave food in a box on someone's doorstep? Well, it would be less work, and it would fill the belly, but you would miss the person—the person who wants to go shopping, choose what he or she wants to eat, get filled up on respect.

All people matter to God, but at Imago we continue to see that the *people in the margins are the first ones we should go to.* Christ went to those whom the comfortable and powerful had rejected. Undoubtedly, He could have been a lot more successful and efficient if He'd gone to the influential people first. But He said He came to seek and to save those who were lost. Christ went to the margins for a reason. He was critiquing the way humans do life. He was saying, "You're missing out." Since many of us fashion our lives to avoid marginalized people, a ministry simply becomes a way to take Christ followers to people and places we'd ordinarily miss.

We're also seeing that *community is an indispensable strength.* There are no lone rangers in the kingdom of God. Jesus sent the disciples out in groups of two. Even talented, well-intentioned people who try to go solo set themselves up for failure. We're all part of a greater entity—the body of Christ. We're deeply dependent on Him for our life, and we receive that life most fully when we gather together before God. We gather to listen to His Word, to confess our sins, to stand in solidarity with sinful people at the table, recognizing that we all need God's grace. We gather to worship Him, to receive His Spirit, to encourage one another...and to be sent out again. But we need a friend with us when we go.

Finally, we're finding that *the genius of the kingdom is nearly always in simplicity*. We keep asking, What's the need? How can we meet it simply? There might be no simpler or more powerful way to be a signpost for the kingdom than to share a meal together. The meal is another part of our culture where life has been reduced. But as Eugene Peterson notes, all through Scripture we see the meal as a centerpiece of God's activity. There's something beautiful and holy about meals when all of a sudden it's not about the food or the preparation but about the people and the journeys and the conversation and the caring.

What would happen if you put another chair at your table at meal-time and asked God to open your eyes to whom you should invite to join you?

When the church first started, Joe and Andrew started sharing meals. It was a simple plan. Joe took his camp stove down to Sixth and Pine in Portland and started cooking dinner. Dinner was soup because soup was what Joe knew how to cook.

Right away, Joe and Andrew had company for dinner.

The next week, they were back at Sixth and Pine with Joe's stove and soup makings. They had more company this time. They really only had one plan for Joe's camp-stove dinners—to be back at that same street corner on the same day every week to share a meal.

That's what they did. Soon they needed to enlist some friends and their camp stoves to help. The guestlist grew to twenty, then thirty. Once they served a hundred. After a time, Joe and Andrew passed the ministry on to others. Now Bruce and Cathy are making the meals and enjoying new company for dinner and being signposts.

On the corner of Sixth and Pine, the good news of the kingdom is that no one in heaven goes hungry and no one is forgotten.

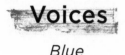

Voices

Blue

It was summer. A dear friend of mine and I were sitting in front of a Starbucks at one of those metal tables that are trying very hard to give the effect of a café in Europe while still looking very American. My friend ordered an iced americano, which quickly caused the plastic cup to be laced in watery jewels. It was an unusually warm day in Oregon. I drank my yerba maté tea that I had brought with me. A gentle wind blew slightly over us. She was struggling with her life. I was struggling with mine. We talked about finding hope in unexpected places. I remember how blue her eyes looked. I remember wondering if she had any idea how amazing and beautiful she really was. As she groped to find hope in her mind and her life, I sat wondering if she realized that at that moment she was giving me hope just by existing. We decided that finding Jesus wasn't all that difficult. It's just that sometimes He seems to hide behind trees and clouds. Other times He is a little more bold and looks at us through human eyes and smiles at us with human lips and teeth. Sometimes He is even so kind as to reach out and touch us. My friend wept from the heaviness of her heart. I reached out to touch her. I hoped that Jesus was hidden somewhere between my fingertips and her shoulder.

—Monique Amado

Sharing the News About Our King

> The Spirit of the Lord is on me, because he has anointed me to preach good news to the poor. He has sent me to proclaim freedom for the prisoners and recovery of sight for the blind, to release the oppressed.

Years ago, some friends were very serious about sharing their faith—bold in ways that I could only wish to be. Once, they picked up a hitchhiker who turned out to be from Germany. After some conversation, they invited her to stay with them in their home.

The first night, we all went out to a great coffee shop in the Hawthorne District. The conversation was light and we were getting to know our new friend. Things turned slightly spiritual when we discussed our backgrounds in church or the lack thereof. Then out of nowhere, my friend asked our visitor if she had ever heard a Christian testimony.

My jaw dropped. I am not sure who was more uncomfortable: our traveler friend or me. "Um, no," she said. "I've never heard of one of those." I was thinking to myself, *Me neither.* I hadn't heard someone refer to their personal journey with Christ as if it were an official document.

But in the split second between her response and my confusion, my friend turned to me and said, "Rick, tell her your Christian testimony."

Somewhat in shock, I turned to my wife for help, but she only smiled at me as if to say she somehow loved the awkwardness and it was only going to get better.

I began to talk, stumbling through my life story and how I met Jesus. It sounded rehearsed and awful, and the kind traveler smiled politely until I was finished.

Then she said quite profoundly, "Hmm."

I find that story funny now, but at the time I was not laughing. I remember thinking that this was not the way I heard the Scripture telling us to share our faith. I am all for boldness, but when we bypass relationship, we are missing something key. We weren't street preachers; we were just having coffee. It seemed to me that there were a hundred better ways to speak of Jesus. I figured I had just learned the hard way how not to speak of Him.

Still, we cannot deny that one of the key aspects of participating with Jesus in the kingdom is that we get to announce His reign with joy and invite people to trust this saving and liberating King. I admit the final obstacle many times to sharing our faith is, frankly, us!

So how *do* we announce our King as the way, the truth, the life, and the hope of the world?

The way of Jesus is the path to the Father through the cross. It is a way marked not merely by the sexiness of social justice or global activism. More fully, it is the way in which we all come to know ourselves: through Jesus.

The challenge of finding Jesus is that He is the narrow, unpaved path among hundreds of streets that seem much broader and well traveled. These streets are posted with many signs. Yet follow any of them and you'll end up in one of a hundred tiny cul-de-sacs where you can spend a lifetime. Cul-de-sacs like success, addiction, approval and rejection, and hundreds of others that every heart seeks. They are large, busy streets where lives rush by at a hundred miles an hour.

The heart is always seeking a way, trying to turn off at this road or the next. We tell ourselves, *If I don't find what I'm searching for here, perhaps I'll find it up ahead. Looks like a lot of people over there. Let's go see what is happening...*

In the midst of all this hurry and waste, though, there's an old wooden sign that leads you toward a dirt path. The simple letters read, The Jesus Way. You can't take much with you on this path, maybe not even your car. It seems that many who travel here do so only in small groups. Most travelers you meet happened here out of need or longing or simply by surprise. It is a path that leads through hill and meadow, by quiet streams. It leads, too, into long, arid stretches where you end up shedding all that is unnecessary.

The Jesus Way is the narrow way. Although so many people claim to believe in Jesus, few follow Him. The highways of culture and acceptable religion race alongside with the other streets. The religious roads take you to quick-fix answers and tacky gimmicks and big billboards advertising the next religious oasis that is just a few miles ahead.

I wonder if many people who want to share their faith are traveling on these wider roads. The idea is simple: get off your highway and get onto ours. All you have to do is trust Jesus. You pray a simple prayer and you wake up in a new car with a new life and a new sense of adventure. No one ever seems to ask where Jesus is; they are all too busy getting there, wherever "there" may be.

The problem on the religious highway is that everyone wants to share his or her faith, but no one wants to tell other people about *Jesus*. They feel guilty, embarrassed, or frankly don't know what the difference is between their highway and the others, so why cause a traffic jam?

We spend countless hours driving down religious highways, and nothing ever changes in our lives except the billboards. Others have beer ads; we have books and Bibles and celebrity preachers.

I am here to tell you that you should feel guilty about trying to get someone to drive down that road. In its own way, it also leads to a death.

The Jesus way is a long walk, and it's all about endurance. You can hear the cars in the distance, but what's louder is the crunching of leaves beneath your feet and the chirping of squirrels in the trees above you.

Yet Jesus is on this path with you. He is your guide. He whispers throughout your day that you are on a different way, and the rules of travel here are different too. Your goal is not to see how busy you can make the place. Your goal is to follow Jesus.

When He stops, we stop. When He starts, we start. If He touches a leper, so do we. There are disconcertingly few rules, which—let's admit it—makes travel all the more difficult. Sometimes someone is lying in the road, and we immediately think we need to go around him. But we are behind Jesus, who meanders up to him, gives him His last sip of water, and invites him to join us.

Now we are going even slower, and the cars on the highway sound even more inviting. They are getting somewhere. We're just getting further lost in the woods.

But I've noticed something. After some time of following Jesus in this way, you begin to walk like Him, live like Him. You want to stop for the hurting fellow traveler. You want to share your last sip of water. You don't know when you changed, but you did.

Eventually, almost everything is changing. Your pace is now a rhythm. The cars no longer excite you, your heart is softened, and you notice what Jesus notices. You are saddened by what saddens Him. Your joys are His joys. In fact, you don't mind at all when other travelers join you, be they wounded from a car wreck or dizzy from circling the cul-de-sac or just arrogant hikers who feel they know how to do this better than Jesus Himself. When He sends you over to the highway to invite others to join you, you are not ashamed or embarrassed this time, because now you know the Jesus way is the better way.

If you are not following Jesus down this path, you should feel guilty about sharing about that faith, giving your Christian testimony. Most likely, it is not the Jesus way.

What way are you taking?

The Jesus truth is a transforming truth. He realigns our lives with what is right. He heals our wounds. We don't simply share the facts and figures of a Jewish rabbi who hung on a Roman cross in the Middle East thousands of years ago. We share how that rabbi is confronting, converting, and re-creating our view of the world all these years later.

The Jesus truth sits among the myriad other truths that are there for the taking. What makes it stand out are the people it keeps reinventing: addicts who have been made clean, greedy people who have learned generosity, selfish people who have become loving, and smart people who have become humble.

These people are like trees planted by a flowing stream, as the psalmist says. People who have gone to the Jesus cross and wept over their sin and kneeled in repentant prayer. There they felt the hand of Jesus upon their shoulders, beckoning them to rise as saints.

This is the truth that *is* Jesus not simply *about* Jesus. This truth opens blind eyes and raises to life those who long ago ran out of gas on the highways of culture and religion. To share this truth you are not reduced to sneaky tactics or sleight of hand or polished speeches. You simply and boldly proclaim the Jesus truth of a loving God who died and rose again. You have been captured by His love and are forever changing in it. You can't help talking about it.

Many people have problems sharing this truth because they themselves have not experienced it or have chosen to not live by it. Guilt shows up listing oughts and shoulds until you quit listening. Guilt is appropriate if you choose to share the truth about Jesus without living it.

But if the Jesus truth is breaking or healing your heart day after day, then pointing this truth out to others is not a response to guilt but a natural act of worship.

The Jesus truth changes everything.

The Jesus life is presently at work in those who follow in the Jesus way and live by the Jesus truth. Birthed by the Spirit of God, it rebuilds what is broken, mends what is ripped apart, and forgives and forgets all your failures.

The Jesus life is not the pristine glamour of gorgeous models you see on billboards. Nor is it clean, a litter-free roadside of the religious highway.

Rather, the Jesus life is something that's re-creating us from the inside out. It is seen in men who are learning to love their wives and adore them, learning to provide and to protect and to cherish them as if they were their first loves. It is seen in wives who are growing to respect their husbands. It is seen in young people who are striving for sexual purity. It is seen in young men who are preparing themselves to enter into marriage by becoming lovers of Jesus instead of youthful freedom. It is seen in young women who are building inner beauty and character in a culture that mocks the thought of such things. It is seen in families learning to be small communities of the Jesus life to one another. Learning to forgive, pray, care, serve.

People on the Jesus way, living by the Jesus truth in the Jesus life, see their whole lives through the rearview mirror of grace. The Jesus life calls us to leave the things that distract us from our hearts and to remember the things we want to avoid so that Jesus can redeem the whole story, not just the parts we offer up. So the Jesus life has times of sadness as we weep at the tomb of our friend, as we weep over cities that reject Jesus, as we weep before a cross we are asked to carry ourselves. The Jesus life is a transforming life that displays the grace, patience, and love of Jesus.

So how does what I've been saying here apply to how we share the news of the King? When we don't live the Jesus life, sharing our faith becomes a history lesson we read about in an ancient book or that the people at our club have decided is an important advertisement we need to get out. It makes us feel guilty because the life that we live is not a life of worship but a play we are acting out called Christianity.

There are a thousand conversations taking place every day between people living the Jesus way, truth, and life and those on the other high-ways. The Spirit of God may or may not turn the conversations into op-portunities for you to share your faith. When He does, you are not sharing *the* faith but *your* faith. Everything you say will come out of what you know and who you are. If you are following Jesus on the narrow path, your life will back up what God puts on your heart to share. If not, then you are likely to shrink back in guilt, arrogantly bash them with your Bible, or simply shrug them off as more sinners getting their due, or, worse, you will not care one way or the other.

The hurdle we are trying to overcome is how we will answer the question, "Will you share your faith with me?" If I could go back in time to the visit with the German traveler at the sidewalk café, I think I would share something different. Perhaps more important, I think she might ask me different things.

Something more like, Would you tell me...

- about the time Jesus got you out of bed and brought you to church so you could hear about His love?
- how He forgave you of all your selfishness and sin?
- how you met your wife and you saw His hand at work in your relationship?
- about your children and what you dream for them?
- about how Jesus held you up when your parents got divorced?
- how He met you in the hospital every time your kids have had a problem?
- how He comforted you when your friends died, how He met you in the dark nights of doubt?
- how He gently invited you to give up control over things and people so you could love?
- how He graciously and patiently kept pursuing you when you failed Him time and time again?
- how He helped you get your act together so you could be the dad and husband your family needed?
- how He walks with you each day in your marriage and helps you two to keep loving, repenting, and forgiving?
- how you met Him in the pain of your past that you have spent your whole life trying to forget and avoid?
- how He is redeeming things inside you that you thought were so unspeakable?
- how He has taken away your shame and restored your value?

- how He has molded your edges and is rebuilding your life?
- how He nudges you to use your money for others instead of things?
- how He has provided for your family beyond what you could ever ask and how He helped you in the moments you thought your bank account would tank?
- how He holds you every week when you weep over the things that break your heart?
- how He beckons you with mercy to follow in His way, His truth, and His life for another day?

These are the questions people truly want answered. The answers have the power to impact, persuade, and convince—rather than turn off or bore the hearer.

If God prompts us into these conversations, we can share our faith and invite others to trust the One who loved them enough to die and rise again. We can participate in sharing the news about our King: His way, His truth, and His life.

10

Welcome the Child

> He called a little child and had him stand
> among them. And he said: "I tell you the
> truth, unless you change and become like
> little children, you will never enter the king-
> dom of heaven."

Another warm spring night has settled over your neighborhood, draping the trees and the bushes in shadows. Yellow light streams from the kitchen window. A firefly or two start blinking and bobbing over the grass. You? You're four or five. This is your yard. You and a bunch of sweaty friends are playing hide-and-seek. In the dark, you're a pirate, a hoot owl, the mighty Aslan about to roar. You plan to play forever and be invisible most of the time, maybe hide in the hydrangeas with Bridget from next door. Maybe. On and on you play in darkness... Then Mom calls, and it's time to go in for bed.

What is it about kids? They're innocent and selfish, sweet and annoying, mysterious and simple. Back when you were a preschooler, you knew stuff you've forgotten now. But how exactly *did* you see and experience the world then? If you could recapture it now, could it help you see and experience the kingdom Jesus preached?

Jesus thought so. In fact, on three separate occasions in Matthew's account, children take center stage. In this chapter, I want to look at these scenes. I think you'll discover that children provide us with something like a portal into important truths about the kingdom experience.

Scene 1: The disciples come to Jesus with a very adult question: Who is greatest in the kingdom of heaven?

We might be tempted to say, "Obviously the guys were just being competitive and immature again," and dismiss the question. But we might also hear their concern as a step of faith. They were thinking seriously about the kingdom, and they cared about how Jesus measured success there.

In reply to their question, Jesus calls a little child to stand among them. "I tell you the truth," He told His followers, "unless you change and become like little children, you will never enter the kingdom of heaven."

The word *change* here actually means to be converted, to become a different kind of person with a different worldview. Jesus is saying, "Change, become childlike, or what you want is not going to happen." He continued,

> Therefore, whoever humbles himself like this child is the greatest in the kingdom of heaven.
>
> And whoever welcomes a little child like this in my name welcomes me. But if anyone causes one of these little ones who believe in me to sin, it would be better for him to have a large millstone hung around his neck and to be drowned in the depths of the sea....
>
> See that you do not look down on one of these little ones. For

I tell you that their angels in heaven always see the face of my Father in heaven.

What do you think? If a man owns a hundred sheep, and one of them wanders away, will he not leave the ninety-nine on the hills and go to look for the one that wandered off? And if he finds it, I tell you the truth, he is happier about that one sheep than about the ninety-nine that did not wander off. In the same way your Father in heaven is not willing that any of these little ones should be lost.

I don't see anywhere here that Jesus is saying that children are perfect little cherubs. Innocent and vulnerable, yes. Sinless, no. Who they are and what they possess of the kingdom does not come by perfection or pride or striving or smart, self-protective scheming. Yet their angels in heaven have direct access to God, Jesus says. Whenever children take foolish risks, the shepherd of heaven comes eagerly and joyfully to their rescue. Children don't have to manipulate care from God; He initiates it.

"Want to really take in My kingdom?" Jesus says to His followers. "Become like this child standing in front of you. He is precious to Me."

Change. Humble yourself. Become like you were those evenings when you played on and on in the shadows just at the edge of the yellow light streaming from home.

Become like Joseph, my neighbor.

Joseph is eighteen months old, and one of his favorite things to do, as far as Jeanne and I can tell, is to fly down the driveway naked after a bath. He holds himself inappropriately and giggles and grins from ear to ear. Fat, freshly scrubbed, and gleeful. Joseph galloping naked across his own personal planet.

You oughta see it.

Of course, if I saw Jeff, his dad, behaving that way, I'd think he needed help. But with Joseph, it's different. The kid is innocent. He's the prince of bathlings, the great khan of his own driveway, and he knows it. Plus he knows that Mom is watching out for him. Joyfully watching. Why *not* take a butt-naked risk? No wonder he wears a perma-grin.

I've noticed that beautiful look on Jeff and Shanti at times, but only in their best moments. They're grownups, after all, like you and me, not toddlers. Life isn't usually cute for grownups. We don't get to make a run for it down the driveway, grabbing ourselves. We're long past those magical evenings of playing in the dark with Bridget and then running in to bed. Outside is a criminal waiting to rip us off. Inside is a person or situation that makes us grind our teeth and think murderous thoughts.

So what could Jesus mean? we wonder. *We don't get it.*

Well, I don't think the disciples quite got it either, because after Jesus' teachings about such adult topics as forgiveness, divorce, and remarriage, the toddlers show up again to provide another learning opportunity.

Scene 2:

> Then little children were brought to Jesus for him to place his hands on them and pray for them. But the disciples rebuked those who brought them.
>
> Jesus said, "Let the little children come to me, and do not hinder them, for the kingdom of heaven belongs to such as these." When he had placed his hands on them, he went on from there.

Notice that the disciples see the children as intruders. But Jesus says, "Don't hinder the children. Forget your schedule and everybody else's expectations. Just let them rush inappropriately right into the middle of things and stare rudely up into My face."

I think of all the ways I hinder my kids. I hinder them by thinking I need to teach them, and teach them right away, all the things they don't know about God. Now, I'm not telling you not to teach your kids about God. But this passage suggests a bigger picture than most of us parents have most of the time. This passage is saying that my kids already understand something about the kingdom that I don't get. So as I download biblical facts and eternal truths into their restless minds, I also need to humbly learn from them.

Why feel chagrined if they run around naked, smiling and giggling and playing in the dirt?

If I threw my son Bryce into an algae-ridden pond, he wouldn't want to leave. He could be there for hours, capturing polliwogs, poking insects, collecting sticks, happily carried along on the pulse of creation.

Afterward, if I asked him, "What did you learn about God?" he'd probably say the obvious: "God is big" or "God likes bugs."

But maybe I should play with him and then ask, "What did *I* learn about God?" Because Bryce isn't missing God. I am the one who should be the careful student in this moment.

An adult would ask, "If the kingdom already belongs to children, how can we create and encounter the kingdom of God with our kids and through their eyes?"

In our church community, we're working out an idea we call Learning Labs. The labs are firsthand explorations of the basic life processes intended to bring children and adult mentors together to think, experience, question, and create. We want to instruct our children in the truths of the kingdom, but we also want them to instruct us.

What could that look like?

Well, if they're learning about creation by playing with worms and dirt, I can observe them digging into the dirt with joy and wonder. They touch and play with the worms—activities I long ago decided to avoid. The children learn from their mentor that God created worms to play a key role in tending the soil. But *I* learn from the children that creation is to be touched and felt and played with. I walk away wondering how I can get back to where they are, to play and touch and feel again. If you tried the same lesson with a PowerPoint or a flannelgraph, you'd kill the experience.

On any given week in Learning Labs, children might be exposed to gardening, pottery making, preparing food for the poor, looking through microscopes at how cells divide and develop into life, meeting and interacting with refugee children and their parents, hearing their mentors' testimonies, or studying trees at the park. Family devotions from each class are posted on the Web, and parents are encouraged to learn along with their children.

The best learning adventures appeal to the whole person, not just the mind. For example, we've noticed that if you say, "Billy, create because you were created," nothing significant happens. But when a mentor leads (or follows) Billy into an experience of creativity—when Billy *does* it— he's back in Genesis and living the creation story. And so is the mentor. The first approach is putting forth a proposition, which churches have tended to focus on to the exclusion of the second approach, which is to invite people into a holistic adventure.

Our dream at Imago is that you would come to church with your kids and travel through Learning Labs as families. Think about it. What if you walked into a church, and instead of seeing a sign that says Sixth-Grade Girls, you saw signs inviting your family to the garden, a science lab, an art studio, a media room, and on and on? If the kingdom is being expressed in all of life, why wouldn't that kind of church school make perfect sense? In the bigger picture, how can followers of

Jesus influence literature and the arts, life sciences, technology, and many other arenas if we've abandoned them because we disagree with what's happening there?

We want to reclaim the wonder of learning for our children—and for ourselves—and help the next generation grow into bold, respected scholars and citizens. We want to graduate what Dallas Willard calls "fully discipled disciples"—followers of Jesus who can, for example, enter into the mainstream scientific community and exert influence for good, who can become for their generation not dissenters but leaders, seekers of truth doing great science.

Interestingly, right after Jesus calls the children to Him and blesses them, He meets a candidate for Mr. Perfect Disciple. He's a poster adult for adultness. This guy has it all—he's rich, educated, unfailingly ethical, and extremely devout. He wants to know how to live forever in the kingdom of heaven. "What good thing must I do?" he asks.

But Jesus tells him that to find treasure in heaven, the man must first put down all his accomplishments and all his possessions. Strip down to just him. "Then come, follow me," Jesus says.

At that, Mr. Perfect turns away sad. It's not what he was prepared to hear.

Do you see the contrast? To the little ones who bring nothing, Jesus says, "Come to Me just as you are." To the adult arriving with everything, Jesus says, "First, drop all of that. Then come."

If you had been a disciple that day, watching the kids playing happily in Christ's presence and watching a man who had everything leaving disappointed, how would you have responded? I think I would have been processing like mad. And not very successfully. *Well, it sounds nice, but how does that help me?* I'd be muttering. *He wants me to be like a kid…the kid belongs to the kingdom. But I'm not a kid, I don't even know how to be a kid, and I don't want to make a bare-naked jerk of myself trying.*

The disciples that day had similar thoughts. In utter confusion, they asked Jesus, "Who then can be saved?"

Jesus answered, "With man this is impossible, but with God all things are possible."

One way I take that statement is that I must put aside my endless striving and open my life in childlike simplicity and utter poverty to what only God can do. And what if God wants to provide *through* a child?

One day, Cece, a young woman with a passion for wildlife conservation, came to lead a lab despite the fact that she suffers terribly in front of an audience. Karen, our children's ministry director, and others had planned and prayed with Cece in advance. Still, when she arrived for the lab, she was shaking. But God met her need through Preston, a boy in the class. Preston must have faced social problems of his own, because as soon as the topic for the day was announced, he launched into a report to Cece about his animals and how much he liked to learn about wildlife. Then he jumped into his questions. Before long, Cece and her young student were engaged in a passionate conversation.

What started as an interruption actually invited two miracles: both mentor and student relaxed, and the rest of the class was pulled into a fascinating and memorable learning experience.

Scene 3: Jesus is just days away from His death on the cross. Jerusalem is swept up in the celebrations of Passover, and Jesus is making a scene in the temple courtyard.

He has just kicked out all the moneychangers and peddlers. Everybody's yelling and running around. Tables are upside down, papers are blowing away, coins are rolling everywhere. Escaped doves flap all over the place. Security guards arrive in a huff.

And Jesus is standing there with a message. "My house will be called a house of prayer," He says. "But you are making it a 'den of robbers.'" Then this happens:

> The blind and the lame came to him at the temple, and he healed them. But when the chief priests and the teachers of the law saw the wonderful things he did and the children shouting in the temple area, "Hosanna to the Son of David," they were indignant.
>
> "Do you hear what these children are saying?" they asked him.
>
> "Yes," replied Jesus, "have you never read, 'From the lips of children and infants you have ordained praise'?"

I love that scene. Upset capitalists. Upset clergy. Upset tables and birds. In the middle of it all, I can hear shuffling. It's the marginalized people of the city getting closer to Jesus for His healing touch. And I hear another sound rising above the noise. The voices of children worshiping God.

They're the only ones who get it.

One Sunday we planned a child-led service. We knew from the beginning that we weren't shooting for a sweet event with children's choirs and proud parents sneaking photographs. We wanted something different. At the beginning of the service, I talked about Jesus' respect for children in His kingdom and then announced that we were going to follow our children into worship.

I invited all the kids to join me on the stage for a story. My prop was a bag of cherries that we ate to find the seed in them. I'm no Mr. Rogers, but the cherries helped. I talked about how Jesus taught that the kingdom of God was like a seed that a farmer plants and it grows into a huge tree in which the birds live. We talked together about how seeds die and then life comes from them and how even a small seed can produce fruit the size of a watermelon or a tree the size of a cherry tree. Then we applied that to how the kingdom could grow in our lives—how some things need to die in the dirt so God can bring new life. And finally we talked about Jesus. He was willing to die so each of us could have new life forever.

"I wonder how it makes you feel to know God loves you like that," I said. "I wonder what you could create to show us how you feel."

We invited them to paint or draw their responses on a huge blank canvas on the platform. (For the younger children, we had set up play areas with clay and chalk and blocks.) While the children played and painted what they were learning, the rest of us watched and learned and sang our worship. What unfolded before us was the story of the children's hearts. During worship the kids blew bubbles, danced, some did cartwheels and splits. Everyone was smiling. Who hasn't wanted to do cartwheels on stage during worship?

At the table, children served.

Have you received communion from a beautiful eight-year-old girl who looks at you with eyes of wonder? "This is the body of Christ, broken for you," she says, holding up a piece of bread.

In a flash, you know what Jesus meant when He said, "The kingdom of heaven belongs to such as these."

What point of pride is keeping you and me from seeing a kingdom that is already here, right next to our skin? What invulnerability?

What silly fear is keeping us from rushing into His inner circle or doing cartwheels for His pleasure?

What religious pose is passing for authentic spiritual connectedness? Let us more carefully consider the children who stand among us. Let us more thoughtfully listen.

These little ones are mysterious beings who, in important ways, are already living what you and I long for. When we go to church, we want so much for God to come and connect with us that we make sure to leave the kids in the pink room downstairs. That way we can pay attention. (Wouldn't want to miss the moment God finally shows up, would we?)

But Jesus flips the whole thing upside down, like He did with those tables in the courtyard. "My kingdom is already here," He says. "Check out the pink room."

Voices

Sylvan's Request

"Will you color with me?" asked Sylvan.
"Not right now, I'm going to go do..."
something important.
I went to do something I needed to do, didn't I?
Oh no.
What a glorious invitation I passed on today.
I could have colored!
I never color anymore.
I saw I wasn't good at coloring, so I stopped.
Growing up is dangerous like that.
It's so easy to forget that playing isn't competing,

so easy to confuse the serious with the important
or the skillful with the valuable.
Sylvan wanted to color while Leo played in a
       cardboard box
and Violette carefully balanced a pillow on her
       head.
How silly they are.
How wonderfully, worshipfully, beautifully silly!
But me?
Well, I had to do something important.

                        —Nathan Bubna

11

Alive in a Million Mysteries

> Look at the birds of the air; they do not sow
> or reap or store away in barns, and yet your
> heavenly Father feeds them. Are you not
> much more valuable than they?

> [Christ is] the firstborn over all creation.
> For by him all things were created: things
> in heaven and on earth, visible and invisible,
> whether thrones or powers or rulers or au-
> thorities; all things were created by him and
> for him. He is before all things, and in him all
> things hold together.

Picture a field of living things awake in the evening, pulsing with a million mysteries. Trees, flowers, grasses leaning. Frogs and foxes. A nighthawk swooping in the dusk overhead. Picture a man and a woman there, listening, talking, alive in the ordinary miracle and waiting. Waiting for what? For the King of the field of living things to come.

Right there I think I lost you. "That's Eden. A story of naked people in a perfect environment. Nice...but *so* not real."

But what if we were willing to journey into creation wearing the lenses of the kingdom? Would we encounter the natural world in a different way? Is it possible, for example, that those million mysteries are still happening and that the King of the field is still King today?

This chapter will explore the way in which God's reign shines through creation and how He calls His kingdom revolutionaries to find creation as a place of worship, a place to represent redemption, the place where we strive to receive and to steward, not simply consume.

Without a doubt, creation *is* scarred by sin. Our attitudes about it are scarred too. But even in the brokenness of creation, beauty shines through. Everywhere we see the fingerprints of God. Just think of a snow-covered mountain or the pink in the morning sun. Think of the silky petals of a rose quietly unveiling color and fragrance.

At Imago, we want to receive His beauty. We want to engage creation from a kingdom perspective and practice the presence of our King within it.

I remember sitting down with Tim and Anna. They have a huge love for the outdoors. Any chance they get, they haul their three kids to the hills and drink in the miracles. What I had in mind was an odd request: Would they dream with me about taking worship at Imago Dei outside the walls of the church?

It didn't take much dreaming before Tim and Anna were chasing some ideas. They started something called the Worship Learning Experience. Several Sundays a year they lead people in an experience of creation that draws them to worship the King and celebrate their connection to His kingdom.

Sometimes they take church to the coast to surf. They wrap this experience in reading psalms and meditating on the power of God. I have spoken at surf worship. There we are on the beach—the Pacific rolling in around the headland, sending wave after wave crashing onto shore. We're talking about the fear of God, about His power as we've just experienced it in the waves. We talk about His beauty as the sun sets. All the while in the soil of our hearts, the mustard seed of kingdom awareness grows. We are learning that the King reigns over all of life and that worship is a 24/7 experience.

Once, the Worship Learning Experience was to clear out a mess of blackberry vines that had overtaken a hillside. Then we replanted the hill with young trees. After several thorn-lashed hours of blood and sweat, the worshipers sat down for bag lunches on the side of the reclaimed hill. Tim pointed around the circle at the muddy knees, sweaty brows, and scratched arms. "This is the gospel," he said.

The gospel in mud and sweat and berry vines? Jesus thought so. In our time, we have become strangely cut off from the natural world. Creation over there, people here. Earth down here, God up there. But when Jesus taught about His kingdom, His listeners suffered from no such dualisms. He used pictures of a natural world they felt a part of: seeds, soil, flowers, fish, fruit trees and thornbushes, sheep and wolves, rain. They understood the creation miracle was continuing: the rhythm of the seasons, the cycles of planting and harvest, the interdependence of man and plant and animal. The breath of God. From dust to dust.

So I think they would have received Jesus' examples from nature with greater impact than most hearers today. Words like:

[Your Father] causes his sun to rise on the evil and the good, and sends rain on the righteous and the unrighteous.

Look at the birds of the air; they do not sow or reap or store away
in barns, and yet your heavenly Father feeds them. Are you not
much more valuable than they?

See how the lilies of the field grow.

I can see them nodding. "Yes, of course. A caring God is intimately
involved in the world He created. He is here. His miracle is continuing.
And we are participants."

But I wonder how Christians today would receive the same teachings.
Some, I think, would immediately argue, "Actually, the sun doesn't rise. It
just looks that way because of the earth's orbit." Some would draw a blank.
"Actually, I've never seen a lily in a field." Many more would probably ask,
"Why the nature lesson when Jesus is talking about spiritual things?"

The larger challenge we face today is that so many evangelicals aren't
really participating in creation at all. They're putting in their time as
aliens in the natural world while they wait for the real show to begin: the
Lord's return, judgment, eternity.

In his book *Christ Plays in Ten Thousand Places,* Eugene Peterson
tells the story of growing up in a beautiful valley in Montana. Every Sunday, the Peterson family would stop by to give their neighbor, Sister Lychen, a ride to church. She was an already small and rapidly shrinking
widow in her nineties. During the service, Sister Lychen would, without
fail, stand up to testify that the Lord had told her she would not die until
He returned. After the service, she would ride home with the Petersons
and retreat to her house, where she would spend the week behind drawn
shades. Sometimes young Eugene would be sent next door by his mother
with a plate of cookies. Over cookies and milk, the two would visit. Sister
Lychen had a formidable grasp of Scripture, especially verses relating to
heaven. But the shades stayed drawn.

Next Sunday, she would stand to repeat her pronouncement.

Peterson, who was nine or so at the time, began to worry. He started calculating how much time he had left. What were the chances he would get old enough to have his driver's license? to kiss a girl? Not great.

The day came when Sister Lychen died. At her funeral, Eugene felt worried and confused. But no one mentioned the deceased woman's weekly prophecy. The world went on as usual.

Peterson describes a fantasy of what might've happened if he could go back as a boy and meet Sister Lychen again: "This day, in my fantasized scenario, while she is in the kitchen getting the milk, I let up the blinds from all the windows. As she returns with the milk, I exclaim, 'Sister Lychen, look! The world!'"

The startled woman drops the milk and shatters the glass. Then, as he imagines it, the young Peterson takes Sister Lychen by the hand and leads her outside and down a trail to one of his favorite destinations—a swamp. He shows her turtles, frogs, nesting birds, a deer leaping from the cattails. They watch as creation happens in them and around them.

The experience changes Sister Lychen. The next Sunday at church, instead of declaring what she knows of death and the end times, she talks about the wonders she's seen in the swamp. "I'm not sure I want to leave and 'be with the Lord' yet," she announces and takes her seat.

I see her as a picture of many contemporary Christ followers, especially in evangelical circles. To them, planet Earth is broken by sin; one day it will be replaced. (Implication: natural resources are meant to be consumed at whatever pace we want and let our grandkids ride bikes if need be.) To them, time is only something that takes us closer to eternity. (Implication: getting serious about environmental stewardship only makes sense for those who don't believe in heaven.) Meanwhile, might as well keep the shades drawn.

Taken as a whole, the gospel of Jesus invites us to yank up the shades on our world. All of creation is a portal that we can look through to witness how the kingdom of God continues to arrive. Key Bible texts suggest three important perspectives on creation for Christ followers:

The first is about ownership. As Genesis 1 opens, God makes a claim on the universe—He made creation; *creation belongs to God.* "In the beginning God…" Out of His eternal existence, He began to create. He said, "Let there be," and it was. Light, oceans, sky, continents, all teeming with life.

Then God stops to rest.

As you follow the story of God's people in the Old Testament, you see Him creating the same rhythm in their week. For six days they are to work in this garden of life—this creation where He places them—and then, on the Sabbath, they will stop to rest. They stop for more than physical rest, though. Part of Sabbath rest is to remember and reconnect with a larger truth: you are tending the garden of another. God reigns as King over all living things. Creation is His possession, His story. Remember.

Second, we see in Scripture that *we are part of creation, and it is part of us.* Because of "in the beginning God created," we are all here. Ultimately, we can't analyze the natural world from a distance. We are *in* it, like fish in water. God immersed us in the biosphere and tasked us with providing for its well-being.

An important implication of this fact is that our spirituality and our faith are also woven into the fabric of nature, not separate from it. For God's people in the Old Testament, worship was an extension of the cycles of planting, animal husbandry, and harvest. Every spiritual sacrifice, for example, was rooted in the earth. Only lately have we removed ourselves from that kind of holistic worldview—that somehow we are disconnected not only from other people but from the natural world and even from our own bodies.

Setting aside the matter-versus-spirit dualism of Western thinking opens up new possibilities for the kingdom reality to break in. For example, it helps us realize that spirituality isn't a generalized state that if we can just block out the annoying details, we can attain for a euphoric moment or two. Rather, genuine spiritual experience shows up in a specific person with a specific body. Shelley or Tom, let's say. Maybe Shelley thinks she has too many pimples, and Tom is not as tall as he wants to be. Maybe their circumstances are anything but spiritual or enlightened. But in that nitty-gritty of their own creation—not in a book or an ideal or a thought or anything separate from their physical beings—Shelley and Tom will grow in spirit and truth. In that garden of their being, God says to each of them, as He did to Adam and Eve, "I will come to you there, and we will walk and talk."

Lastly, the New Testament shows us that *Jesus is King of creation*. John opens his gospel by placing the person of Jesus in the context of creation:

He was with God in the beginning.

Through him all things were made; without him nothing was made that has been made. In him was life, and that life was the light of men.

In the letter to the Colossians, Paul goes even further:

[Christ] is…the firstborn over all creation. For by him all things were created: things in heaven and on earth, visible and invisible, whether thrones or powers or rulers or authorities; all things were created by him and for him. He is before all things, and in him all things hold together.

Essentially these texts tell us that not only does the universe belong to God but the universe has been created by Jesus and for Jesus. Every visible thing—from the majesty of mountains to a newborn baby to the complexity of the subatomic world—as well as every invisible power exists because of and for Jesus. Not only that, but "in him all things hold together."

What are you seeing now as you look through the portal of creation into the reality of the kingdom of God? We're talking about some mega shifts in our thinking. I see that I am immersed in a cosmic story that is not about me. Not really.

And yet...

The story I see is of a God who created a universe through and for His Son, Jesus, and that this Jesus is sovereign over it and that, as a participant in the story of creation, I am invited to show forth His kingdom and tell of His glory. I see that I am called to more—to tell the story of a God who pursues what is already His. For as I look into creation, I see a God who came in the flesh to His own garden to reclaim and redeem it from the curse of sin. John wrote,

He was in the world, and though the world was made through him, the world did not recognize him. He came to that which was his own, but his own did not receive him. Yet to all who received him, to those who believed in his name, he gave the right to become children of God—children born not of natural descent, nor of human decision or a husband's will, but born of God.

So the story I am a witness to is both a tale of creation and re-creation. The whole earth is full of the news. Every mountain and swamp and Tom and Shelley declare it. The King has come to enter our mess, to pursue His own, and by the sacrifice of His life, to bring us new life in Him.

Beautiful.

What would happen if hundreds of people descended onto the town or city where you live to redeem creation with the love of the King? What would happen if people who did not follow Jesus were invited on the journey? What if they tasted the kingdom in creation, in the sweat of redemption, and when it was all over, you could explain why it moved their souls—because the King loves them more than the flowers they planted and He proved it with His own death? What would it look like if we practiced the kingdom by creating sacred space all over our cities and towns by simply redeeming the mess of creation with the beauty of restoration?

Let me share some stories from my community, where we are wrestling humbly and hopefully with just such questions.

Meet my friend Peter. He's a big guy with a snakeskin eye patch over one eye. Peter thinks every follower of Christ is called to be an environmentalist. He doesn't think, for example, that the Genesis mandate of human dominion over the biosphere has anything to do with pillage, profit, or selfish consumption. Peter was a pastor until he took a sabbatical and went on a thousand-mile hike with a couple of pack llamas. That experience of wildness ruined him in the best way. Peter came home, resigned from his position, and started an organization called Restoring Eden.

Here is Restoring Eden's mission, from their website: "to make hearts bigger, hands dirtier, and voices stronger by rediscovering the biblical call to love, serve, and protect God's creation." Restoring Eden lives out the biblical mandate to "speak up for those who cannot speak for themselves" as grassroots activists advocating for natural habitats, wild species, and indigenous cultures.

Peter likes to hand out bumper stickers that say "Extinction Is Not Stewardship." When he speaks on college campuses, Peter hauls along a four-hundred-year-old stump. He tells the story of the stump that lived here prior to Columbus and the boys. The story of the stump helps him talk about the difference between stewarding and consuming. His group is active in promoting nature appreciation as a spiritual discipline, caring for the environment, and lobbying. "If we do not speak the truth that God loves His creation, who will?" they ask. Peter isn't motivated by left-wing politics or some new age agenda. He is motivated by the kingdom. He has seen it everywhere in creation, and it has touched his soul.

Peter is helping me learn what it means to be aware and to care and appreciate creation as a sign of the kingdom. I'm learning that we can, for example, stand side by side with environmentalists who are coming at the same issues from other value systems. We don't have to be angry eco-warriors. We can balance environmental commitments with a biblical understanding that creation was given to us to serve us. That doesn't mean we're free to rape the earth; it means we're obligated to love what God loves.

Meet Dan, another friend at Imago. He started a group called Renovo that takes a "simpler is better" approach to creation care. "We ask how we can weigh in on environmental issues in a way that is simple, practical, and makes a positive impact," he says. They promote recycling, carpooling, and bicycling in Portland to reduce dependence on fossil fuels. Simple doesn't mean small, though. "We believe that it is important for us, as members of the kingdom of God, to seek restoration that goes beyond simply slowing down the tide of environmental destruction." The Renovo team is helping Imago learn that creation is part of the kingdom.

Meet Josh and Amanda. Creation restoration is a big deal to them.

They started to dream of what it would look like for Imago to redeem a park on behalf of the community. Saint Francis Park, wedged into a one-block space on Portland's inner east side, had recently become a hangout for drug dealers. In the past, the park had played an important role in the community, but by the time we started to study the possibilities, the park had been shut down for six months after a murder on the property.

Josh and Amanda helped to mobilize the Imago Dei community to sponsor what we called "creating sacred space." (The idea originated with Clint, in Nassau, who told us about how his church had turned a trash-strewn cliff into a place the islanders now come to in the evening to watch the sun go down.) They worked with the city to get the necessary permissions. Then teams from Imago gathered manpower and supplies and prepared us to convene at the park on a Saturday in September.

It was a beautiful event. Hundreds of people worked with wheelbarrows, rakes, and shovels. Many homeless friends worked alongside us since they called the park home. Local artists painted a mural over defaced walls. Children helped to paint another mural inside the park near the playground. Neighbors came out to see what was going on. One woman told us, "I have not seen a kid in that park in ten years." We closed out the day with a huge barbecue and a band.

I have a picture of my son Bryce's hands patting the dirt around a flower he just planted with a homeless man. To me that moment tells the whole story of loving all of God's creation and of reclaiming a space as sacred. What had been a haven for violence and drugs became a place where the kingdom was breaking in, where children were planting flowers with homeless people. The lion was lying down with the lamb.

The idea of creating sacred space continues to grow. It has morphed into an event called Love Portland, in which Imago Dei works with the Palau Foundation and other local churches. Every year, thousands volunteer in a season of service (see ServePortland.org).

We want to keep dreaming. The year after reclaiming Saint Francis Park, the list of projects grew to fifty. Some large, some small, all promising opportunities for us to be agents of the King in this living, breathing garden of His.

I have to ask, What would creation consciousness look like in your life? Different, I'm sure. But the face of caring, guarding, advocating, and restoring *should* be as varied as our opportunities, our persons, and our callings.

What if we let the kingdom of God begin to shape our realities and our stories so that His reign over creation is how we actually see creation, how we actually live?

This is a place to start: to wake up to the million mysteries that unfold in us and around us every day. Why are so many who know God as Father passing their gift of days behind drawn shades? We must come alive. We must say with every breath and with every act, "Look! The world!"

I think we must also vow to fight a fight of faith to keep the universe belonging to Jesus in our hearts and minds. This will take intentionality, because we're all at risk of allowing our lives to be reduced, to instinctively function as if the world is about us and for us, and its Sovereign is absent, and His kingdom is not here.

As we respond in these ways to our moment in His field of living things, we will be cultivating a life of holistic worship, where we can say each day as we pull up the shades and look into one another's faces, "God, You are Lord of creation—and it is very good."

 Voices

Waiting

The sky has grown tired of holding up the trees,
the slow tedium of repetition.
Encircled by winter, all things living
are hungry for the sweet taste of color,
white blossom, green branch on blue sky.

Early on a February morning, a tall maple
weeps quietly, stretching his naked wrists to the sky,
and I wonder at the difference between begging
     and longing,
at the knowledge of created things.
There are times when I can imagine myself with
     a gift
for consolation, and the sky and trees are soothed,
and we all have patience enough for a little more
     waiting.
We tell stories to warm our days with memory,
or let the air fall silent and still.
Our breath turns to lace.
Remembrance is sweetness and aching,
and winter the space in between.

—Sabrina Fountain

12

Stamp of Empire

> Where your treasure is, there your heart will
> be also.

The problem with most followers of Jesus is that we don't care enough about money. We don't get together enough to celebrate the sheer power and pleasure of treasure. It really *is* stunning—what you can do with it, how it makes you feel. When was the last time you heard of a church throwing a wine and cheese tasting party at the top of a skyscraper with this objective: to pull together a bunch of financial freethinkers who are ready to create and spend wealth in a way that puts the kingdom of God first? You have to wonder what that approach to money management would look like. What would it look like, for example, on Wall Street? It would make headlines all over the place—but go mysteriously unnoticed by millions too. Best of all, though, we'd live with a permission slip on this issue. Every day we'd wake up understanding the freedom of knowing whose beautiful likeness is stamped on our money and how to spend it well in His empire. Instead, we slave away for our paychecks, and then spend foolishly, save meagerly, and give guiltily.

Jesus talked a lot about money, but the slave-to-guilt scenario is *not* the new way of living He came to announce. Take this parable, for example:

The kingdom of heaven is like a merchant looking for fine pearls.
When he found one of great value, he went away and sold
everything he had and bought it.

One message I get from this parable of Jesus unfolds like this:

1. You and I are merchants: we're meant to specialize in acquiring,
   caring for, and reinvesting real treasure.
2. You and I are obsessed with treasure: high value totally motivates
   us; low value leaves us apathetic.
3. Not all treasures are created equal.

Clearly the pearl merchant in Jesus' story poured his energy into
tracking down the finest pearls. More than anyone, he knew the value of
the pearl of great price. I imagine that others thought he had gone crazy
when he came back, announced what he'd found, and started cashing in
all his carefully collected chips. There go the camels, the Persian rugs, the
silk shoes. There goes the Benz. The neighbors start talking. The wife
and kids get nervous.

But the pearl hunter operates in a different kind of kingdom. He has
a clear vision of what constitutes lasting, high value, and he pursues it
passionately, single-mindedly, and successfully. Just what is that one pearl
worth? Everything. In the book of Acts, we meet more pearl merchants—
real people this time. They are the new converts to the Jesus way. They,
too, have come upon a treasure of great value, and it has totally rewired
how they think about money and possessions.

Here's the account:

All the believers were one in heart and mind. No one claimed that
any of his possessions was his own, but they shared everything
they had. With great power the apostles continued to testify to
the resurrection of the Lord Jesus, and much grace was upon

them all. There were no needy persons among them. For from time to time those who owned lands or houses sold them, brought the money from the sales and put it at the apostles' feet, and it was distributed to anyone as he had need.

It's sort of like the wine party on the roof; they are practicing the presence of the kingdom with their cash. Something over-the-top crazy and deeply transformational.

The transformation continues today. I wish you could meet my friend Shane. He knows the power of money—thinks highly of it enough to make redistributing wealth a big agenda item for his life. The power of money, for example, convinces him to make the personal choice to live in poverty. Then there are his unconventional efforts to get people to reimagine a kingdom that is not enslaved by the economics of greed.

Some people think he's crazy. I think he is a genius.

For example, he came into twenty thousand dollars recently as a result of a one-time gift in addition to a settlement from a civil lawsuit. The court settlement came after Shane and others had expressed solidarity with New York's homeless by sleeping outdoors with them (long story of wrongful arrest and police misconduct). Shane lives in a faith community among the poor in Philadelphia. So you'd think that when twenty thousand dollars suddenly showed up, he might upgrade his living arrangements or at least buy truckloads of soup and bread for his homeless friends.

But Shane had something more strategic in mind. The money would be returned to the poor, but in a dramatic way. He shares more in his book *The Irresistible Revolution:* "So $20,000 was enough to stir up the collective imagination. What would it look like to have a little Jubilee celebration?" (The Year of Jubilee, according to Leviticus 25, occurred every seven years. All debts were forgiven—a fresh financial start for those in greatest need.)

Working with a coalition of adventurous co-conspirators, Shane took the money and headed for the stock exchange on Wall Street. Their strategic opportunity: the opening bell at the exchange.

The group hid two-dollar bills all over lower Manhattan, lugged in over thirty thousand coins in briefcases and backpacks, and climbed to balconies above the crowd, carrying thousands of dollars in ones. Word spread through the alleys and projects that something was up, and hundreds gathered.

At 8:20 a.m., as the buyers and sellers inside started killing one another to make a buck, Shane and Sister Margaret, a seventy-year-old nun, stepped up to proclaim the jubilee. Their declaration read in part,

> We are a broken people who need each other and God, for we have come to recognize the mess that we have created of our world and how deeply we suffer from that mess. Now we are working together to give birth to a new society within the shell of the old. Another world is possible. Another world is necessary. Another world is already here.

Then, in keeping with Jewish tradition, Sister Margaret blew a ram's horn, and Shane announced, "Let the celebration begin."

Cash started falling from the sky. On the steps, kingdom conspirators dressed as businesspeople, tourists, homeless persons, and passersby started emptying their bags and pockets of change. "The streets turned silver," Shane recalls. "Those who needed money picked it up. Those who didn't put it down. The police looked on in confusion, but the joy was contagious, even for the Wall Street traders." New York was shocked and disarmed to see the evidence of another kingdom breaking in.

But that wasn't all.

Shane and other members of his group sent a hundred-dollar bill to a thousand communities around the world that, in their opinion, incarnate the spirit of jubilee. In the envelope with the money, Shane quoted the verse from Acts about laying money at the apostles' feet.

One of the pastors to receive a hundred-dollar bill from Shane was me. Across the bill he'd written the word *love*. On the day I received it, I put it in my pocket. *Now what?*

I wondered. Sure it was mine now, but I'd received it from one of the poorest guys I know. I knew I had to use it well, but I held on to it for a while.

Every now and then, I'd take my wallet out and see it. The bill didn't look ordinary to me; it felt different, not really mine. It had the stamp of empire on it. *I'm holding a sacred hundred-dollar bill,* I thought. *I don't know if I've ever held one before.*

One day I ended up in a store with no cash, so I pulled out the hundred to tide me over. But it said "Love" all across it, and that's not why I was in the store. Nothing in that particular store had anything to do with love. I put the bill back in my pocket.

By the time Jeanne and I passed the money on to a single mom, we had received a visceral lesson in kingdom economics. Money is to be treasured—but differently.

Because not all treasures are created equal.

Every bill is marked.

Have you ever wondered why people didn't just walk away when Jesus started talking about money? That's the impulse most of us have when an elder stands to announce a new pledge drive or a panhandler hits us up on the sidewalk. But people stayed to hear Jesus, and the crowds grew. In fact, the account of His kingdom teachings ends with this observation: "When Jesus had finished saying these things, the crowds were amazed at his teaching."

Why amazed? I think because what He said stripped away layers of pretense and rationalization and religiosity and went straight to the heart-felt dilemmas of the human experience.

No doubt about it, money is a profound dilemma. How do I value money without being owned and corrupted by it? How do I steward everything I have for God while taking responsibility for putting bread on the table and a roof over our heads? When is my giving, no matter how generous, more about me than someone else?

With money we feel powerful, respectable, and safe—or we think we will if we can just get a little more. Without it, we feel anxious, vulnerable, lost at sea. But money is so powerful and alluring that it can make us into people we hate, doing things we don't respect.

When we look at what Jesus said about money in His kingdom teachings, we see warnings that go to the heart of the dilemma. Jesus said:

Where your treasure is, there your heart will be also.

In another saying, Jesus takes this thought even further: since our hearts follow our treasure, whatever treasure we choose is what we will ultimately serve with our lives. Here's how Jesus sets it out:

No one can serve two masters. Either he will hate the one and love the other, or he will be devoted to the one and despise the other. You cannot serve both God and Money.

You see the trap. Money matters *and* it can be lethal. If you love money for what it can do for you, you will serve it, not God. The evidence is everywhere, maybe even in your own heart.

We could sum up what Jesus' audience heard about money that day like this:

What you look to for freedom and security can actually enslave you. But I am bringing you a kingdom of lasting treasure, a kingdom that has everything you need. I'm inviting you to find your security and freedom in it.

Jesus came to absolutely redefine the role of money in our lives and to release us to be part of what He's already doing in our world. Which leads me to ask, What if you and I spent every bill or coin as if it already carried the stamp of His kingdom? What if we lived in the freedom of knowing that our money is simply a tool in the hands of the King to bring about His goodness and healing? Or if we lived in the freedom of knowing that God could give us as much money as He wanted, yet we'd still choose to serve Him and not money?

What would that kind of freedom look like?

In the kingdom of God, we are called to care, share, and give. While those values might sound like what young moms teach their kindergarteners, they actually reveal the fingerprints of another world. And they are freedom words, I believe, for followers of Jesus.

Let's begin with how we spend. Kingdom care would mean we are willing to ask tough questions about what we do with the dollars in our wallets and in our investments. It would call us to see ourselves not simply as consumers but as agents of the King.

Those two paradigm shifts in our thinking could make an enormous impact.

For example, when we go shopping, we look for deals. That's because we want to be smart consumers and good stewards of what God has given us (and because He hasn't, we think, given us *quite* enough). Most of us don't ask, "Will this transaction be a good deal for everyone?" If the clothing we buy is a bargain because a ten-year-old Malaysian girl worked twelve-hour days seven days a week to make it, how could that be a kingdom transaction? Even if her Malaysian town is happy to have the garment factory, we're called on to be aware of how American corporations along with American consumption habits and requirements are re-shaping lives and cultures in the global economy. Ultimately, if our gain leads to another's loss, a different empire is at work, one not ruled by our King.

A friend of mine makes a point of being socially conscious about his investments. That means, for example, that the portfolios and corporations his funds go to have been thoughtfully evaluated for kingdom values relating to persons, cultures, and the environment. When he heard that a company he had invested in was releasing illegal toxins into the environment, he moved his funds to a more responsible investment until the company remedied the problem. Companies tend to listen to that, and they come into compliance.

Kingdom people would give differently too. We might need to re-think old assumptions.

For example, while donating to charities is a traditional approach to giving, most of the time charities work on principles of financial self-interest—namely, I give you money, you feel better because you received money, and I feel better because I helped you (plus I get a tax deduction). Great things have been done through charities on global, national, and local levels. Nothing is necessarily wrong with that sequence, but kingdom living will move people to deeper, more creative understandings.

For example, kingdom giving nearly always calls us into relationship. By connecting givers and receivers as persons and equals first, both experience something better and higher, and the dignity of both is honored. My friends Bruce and Cathy used to lead one of our homeless ministries at Imago. Every Saturday they'd head to Portland's east side to redistribute wealth. But it comes with the heart of God written on it. I love watching Bruce tell stories about their work. Bruce is a tough guy, but when he talks about the people he's gotten to know on the streets, he chokes up. He does more than pass out supplies he bought with charity dollars; he becomes connected to the homeless as persons. They are not simply homeless; they are people with names and stories. They are Bruce and Cathy's friends. Friends whose needs opened the door for a new mutual relationship.

Giving in the context of relationship also steers us toward giving the kind of help the recipient actually needs, not the help we're guessing they need or that is convenient for us to give. Too often, Christian givers end up patting themselves on the back for a wrong job well done. They might as well have been handing out bowling balls to starving people.

Our community has learned a lot about the relational dimension of giving from Celestin Musekura, a friend from Rwanda. Celestin invited us to understand his people first, then consider helping them in ways that would empower them as persons of worth and ability. When we caught his vision, he proposed that we help him start microbusinesses in Africa. The genius of microbusinesses is that they require partnership with local entrepreneurs but not that much capital from sponsors. We helped Celestin start five businesses for twenty thousand dollars.

One microbusiness idea focused on meeting the needs of adults disabled in the war in Sudan. Doable product idea: manufacture soccer balls for sale to local schools. The idea succeeded. Profits from the first year's sales brought income and paid for materials needed for year two. But the big-picture outcome is even better: a one-time investment empowered some beautiful but previously overlooked people to implement their gifts and creativity to serve a local business opportunity while earning new income.

Working through Celestin has allowed us to participate in an amazing kingdom adventure. Imago has remained in relationship with our new business partners, and we're seeing those one-time gifts reproduce themselves year after year for hundreds of empowered Rwandans.

Consider the revolutionary potential of sharing. What if you and your neighbors started sharing simple things, like a lawn mower. Why do the forty people on your street—who probably live like strangers to one another—all need a lawn mower that will run for only an hour a week? So let's say you and three others shared the same machine. In the process of four people sharing, you would save about six hundred dollars. What could you do for the kingdom with that? Think of the relationship building that would occur naturally while you worked out your plan. Can you afford your own lawn mower? Of course, but you choose to share and to know one another.

What if this sharing gig caught on with the four of you? You could begin to rethink the opportunities to live interdependently with your cars and commuting to work. You could reduce insurance, fuel, payments, and repair costs. Between the four partners, you could be saving an additional five hundred dollars a month pretty quick.

Now what do you do? Well, what if...

What if you make a kingdom connection with Teresa, a single mom in your neighborhood, the one who is raising your son's best friend? Teresa works nights at a low wage and goes to school during the day. What if you and your three sharing partners pooled your sharing-generated dollars to come alongside Teresa in her mission to raise and provide for her son and get herself through school? If you did, a lot of things could change. She and her son would have more time together and experience the love of Jesus in a very direct way. Your neighborhood could celebrate her achievements and spend time together as families. Imagine the day you all go to her graduation. That would be an amazing kingdom moment as she walked across the stage, your son and her son next to you, cheering Teresa on. No amount of cash could buy what you'd be feeling at that moment.

And it all happened because you started sharing a lawn mower.

Which brings us back to wine and cheese, to money falling from the sky in New York City, and to me staring into the face of a sacred hundred-dollar bill.

In our culture, every dollar we carry has a picture on it. The real picture isn't of George Washington or Alexander Hamilton or any American hero. Usually it's of you. Of me. We think we put that dollar in our pocket with our hard work or our good fortune, and we expect to spend it on our wants and wishes.

That is not the kingdom of God. That is the stamp of another empire, and we are bowing to another lord.

What if we saw our money differently, cared about it more, as God cares about our money? As my friend Shane says, we need to conspire creatively together to make space for the kingdom to break in to our lives and our world. In the kingdom, my money is put in my care with the word "Love" written across it.

That leaves only one question that I can see: Who will I love with that dollar, and how?

Voices

Advent

Last summer,
Robert looked at me,
asked how I
in my private college,
white-skin,
rich-family,

suburban-cushioned life
could possibly understand
what it was like
to lose everything,
to have people walk by
pretending to read
the *Wall Street Journal,*
to be so drugged up,
cast out,
written off,
the gum people pull off their shoes—
how could I know
what it was to need,
to breathe, Jesus
with my last breath?
Maybe I am weaker.
Maybe it takes less to get my attention.
Maybe this isn't a contest I want to win.
Silenced, I pulled myself off
the bottom of his shoe,
walked back into my life
of air-conditioned cars
and ten pairs of shoes,
not understanding anything.

—an excerpt, Kristin Mulhern Noblin

13

We Must Go Through
Many Hardships

Blessed are you when men hate you,
> when they exclude you and insult you
> and reject your name as evil, because of
> the Son of Man.

Rejoice in that day and leap for joy, because
great is your reward in heaven.

We must go through many hardships to enter
the kingdom of God.

Ever wonder what story Paul's back could tell? Or his limp? Here is the one apostle who seemed to play the largest role in spreading the good news of the kingdom across his world. But the mission came at a cost. Paul was beaten repeatedly. He was chained in prison. Angry crowds threw stones at him. I think he suffered broken bones, infections, and deformities. His back must have looked like a very ugly topographical map. Here was a man who sold everything for the pearl of greatest price.

Before he ever spoke a word, what story did Paul's presence tell? I think it announced, in the strongest terms possible, the revolution of Jesus—that it was here, authentic, costly, and worth everything. Every welt and lump and scar on Paul's battered body announced the beautiful reality of the kingdom of God.

When we read the stories in Acts of the first disciples, words like *suffering, persecution,* and *martyrdom* quickly come to mind. We shouldn't be surprised. Their stories echo many of the same elements of their leader's story, and Jesus warned that all His followers could expect exclusion, rejection, and insult on His account.

My story isn't like that, though. Is yours?

When I read the accounts of persecution in the early church, I might as well be watching a documentary on the D-day invasion on the History Channel. My mind tells me those things actually happened, but my feelings and imagination treat it like just another story, not the God-announced life trajectory for every Christ follower.

Of course, everyone suffers. I know what it's like to lose a friend, to watch my child suffer, to feel caught in the injustice and pain of a fallen world. And so do you. But the disciples' suffering was different. Stephen was stoned to death for preaching. Peter and John were jailed for healing people. The key distinctive is that these Christ followers *chose* to risk suffering and death rather than live in safety.

Take Paul's experience in Lystra. In Acts 14, we read:

> They stoned Paul and dragged him outside the city, thinking he was dead. But after the disciples had gathered around him, he got up and went back into the city. The next day he and Barnabas left for Derbe.
>
> They preached the good news in that city and won a large number of disciples. Then they returned to Lystra, Iconium and

Antioch, strengthening the disciples and encouraging them to
remain true to the faith.

Did you catch the outrageous danger quotient in the disciples' actions? Even after being stoned and left for dead, they *went back* into the
city. And *preached the good news again.* Before long, they returned to Lystra *a third time* to minister.

In the last sentence in this short account, the two disciples explain
their high-risk behavior:

"We must go through many hardships to enter the kingdom of
God," they said.

Paul and Barnabas were describing an intentional lifestyle. They
didn't have to keep proclaiming the gospel of Jesus and the kingdom.
Paul could have bought a nice little flat in some sweet Mediterranean
town to write his world-changing letters. But he didn't.

That's what I want us to think about together in this chapter: What
is the role of suffering as an intentional lifestyle in spreading the gospel of
the kingdom? Could it be that choosing to suffer accomplishes what
nothing else can? If so, what could my part in suffering look like?

My world is safe. I can drive on a safe, clean freeway to Imago Dei,
speak about the kingdom, celebrate it, relate to the wonders of it, then
walk out on the sidewalk without thinking I need to watch my back. I
can write a book about Jesus or post something on the Web, and no one
comes to arrest me. I enjoy religious and political freedoms. To God and
to those who gave their lives for what I experience, I am grateful.

I notice, though, that my freedoms shape my expectation, and my
expectation is simple and powerful: suffering is to be avoided at all costs.

Even though I want to follow Jesus and I admire Paul and all those who suffered for their faith, I assume (without quite admitting it) that to avoid suffering is both a human and a smart response. In fact, I have a label for people who seek to hurt themselves: masochists. The most suffering I'm likely to encounter on a Sunday morning is that someone might walk out or fall asleep in the middle of my remarks. Even then, shortly after 1 p.m., I know I'll be back on that safe, clean drive home.

Choosing to suffer for the kingdom is, I'll admit, a stretch for me. It's confusing too. The Christians I know who experience persecution talk about going to pray around the flagpole at their high school and risking someone throwing an orange at them. Others who suffer more dramatically (let's say they survive a kidnapping in Afghanistan or Colombia) come home famous. They get on TBN or talk to Katie Couric, book deal already in hand. The American church doesn't produce martyrs; we produce celebrities.

Yet in many other parts of the world, suffering is a way of life for those who follow Christ. For them, the accounts in Acts of disciples getting singled out for persecution or lynched or jailed or pushed into poverty because of their crazy passion to proclaim the gospel read, not like history, but like their life now.

That's why it's clear to me that on the issue of suffering to proclaim the kingdom, Westerners need to look to other places around the globe for insight. We might as well face it: our chance of grasping a realistic theology of suffering for the gospel without help from beyond the West is about nil.

A few years ago, about fifteen friends gathered at my friend Clint's place in Nassau. We were not suffering. We were enjoying great food, tropical sun, and white-sand beaches. Even better was the company—amazing, passionate, humble, subversive servants of Jesus from many different parts of the world. We sat in a circle sharing where the kingdom seemed to be showing up most in our different ministries and areas of interest. Then the talk turned to suffering.

I remember that a few of us from the West seemed to dominate the conversation. Our brothers from elsewhere mostly listened. But I remember something else. When we spoke of it, suffering was an idea. When they spoke of suffering, they shared a big part of their stories.

Cuba came up in the conversation. Someone said the church there, led mostly by women, was thriving but desperately needed medical supplies. How could we get help into a mostly closed country? The idea guys suddenly fell silent. We felt sympathetic but didn't have much to say. At the time, travel to Cuba from the United States was restricted.

Celestin, our friend from Rwanda, spoke up. "What would happen if you took medical supplies to Cuba to your sisters there?"

"You would get arrested," I said. Someone else began to explain to Celestin the embargo and other legal roadblocks. But Celestin interrupted.

"Wouldn't that preach?" he asked.

At first I didn't get what he was saying. I figured he was having trouble translating his thoughts into English. But he said it again.

"Wouldn't that preach to the world if you got arrested while taking medical supplies into Cuba for your sisters?"

At that moment, I felt like I had taken a baseball bat in the ribs. I'd been hit with the dangerous side of the kingdom and, I'm embarrassed to admit, by a thought that never would have come to my mind in a million years. Clearly my creativity for the gospel ended at the point of suffering. Celestin's simple question suddenly seemed rich with revolutionary genius.

What *would* the world think if we loved our sisters in Cuba enough to take them the medicine they needed? How much could our lives say *without speaking* if we were willing to suffer for the sake of the kingdom?

The act alone would preach volumes.

Celestin is no stranger to suffering. He has been imprisoned for his faith in Jesus and for preaching. He has been beaten in those prison cells. In those cells, he has spoken with boldness and compassion to the guards who threatened his life. One of the guards said to him, "We have the tapes of your sermon. We know what you have been saying."

"Good!" Celestin replied. "Did you listen to them? Are you ready to believe? You can kill me—I know where I am going. But I am worried about you."

Celestin told me that when he is in jail, his church thrives. It's a weird paradox. He told me about another pastor who, along with his sons, was maimed and then killed in front of the pastor's wife. But she now leads the church, even though she is illiterate. A boy comes by her home a couple of times a week to read her selected Bible passages. On Sunday she preaches the message she has heard. Her church, too, is flourishing. "You cannot kill the church—you cannot," says Celestin.

Not long ago, Celestin stayed at my home. We walked the hills overlooking Mount Saint Helens and talked. He'd completed another term of study at seminary and was preparing to return to Africa.

I asked him how he dealt with the threats to his safety from his constant travel, both inside and outside Africa. Every time he returns, he risks arrest, beatings, torture, imprisonment. I asked him why he didn't just stay in the States on his student visa. He said, "I would rather die in a jail cell in Sudan, preaching the gospel to my enemies, than on Highway 75 in Dallas."

He added, "Rick, my family knows what I am doing. They are committed to the good news of the King and His kingdom coming to my people. My twelve-year-old son has told me, 'Father, it will be okay if you die preaching Jesus, because we have God as our Father.'"

Conversations with a disciple like that can rock you to the core. In

Celestin's life, I see so much beauty and a willingness to suffer in the mess for the sake of his King. I, on the other hand, am the guy who doesn't want to go to India because I could get an upset stomach. I might suffer in the heat. My mind likes to think of ways to strategically avoid suffering. But Celestin's life is about strategic suffering.

The act itself preaches.

It is not my fault that I was born in the West. I don't need to feel guilty about that, but rather I receive it in gratitude. Still, I notice another way that my freedoms shape my assumptions: I have felt superior to those who suffer.

It is an ugly truth. I have subconsciously assumed that their suffering is due to their inferiority—they have pulled a sort of second-class seating assignment in God's big blue kingdom bus. Facing that shameful prejudice has been a harsh awakening for me and has required a lot of repentance. If it's not my fault that I was born in the West, then neither is it to my credit. Celestin's son would cry as hard if his father were killed as my son would cry if I were killed. Those mothers in the refugee camps in Darfur hurt the same way a mother in Iowa would hurt if she were watching her child slowly starve to death.

During another conversation at Clint's, I was struck by our global friends' compassion toward the Western church. In many ways, they feel sorry for us. They see our arrogance toward the rest of the world, our addiction to pleasure and comfort, our culture of sensuality and excess, which make it hard for us to fathom many of Christ's teachings. They see these not as evidence of superiority but as proof of disadvantage and poverty. They mourn our deep losses and have told us that they pray for us about these things.

"We see what you're up against," Celestin said. "When you have medicine for the dandruff in your hair and for the fungus in your fingernails, it's hard to believe that you need God on a daily basis. That's a difficult thing to be up against."

C. René Padilla, a theologian from Central America, looked at us and said, "We love you. We love the church in the West, and we're praying for you." But he said it as if we had a bigger problem than they did.

Praying for *us*? Another baseball bat to my rib cage. How right these "have not" friends are about the spiritual poverty of the "have it all" world.

I left the circle of conversation thankful that at least some who see us clearly for what we are and who we are not are praying for us.

In our faith community at Imago Dei, we are on the slow road of learning about how suffering is an integral part of practicing the presence of the kingdom.

First, we are seeing that we need to suffer with those who suffer.

If your wife were dying of cancer, you would suffer with her. You wouldn't just show up once a month with flowers and a nice card. You would think about her day and night. You would weep with her. You would spend time with her. You would labor in prayer for her and ask others to do the same. You would pursue every option you could think of to help her carry the burden of her illness.

Suffering with others around the globe may look different than we instinctively think it does. For example, suffering with them doesn't necessarily mean rushing in to fix their problems for them. In fact, our friends who live in the midst of suffering have told us that fixing the problem is not necessarily their goal for us either. What they desire more than money or programs or American know-how is relationship. Relationship means more than reading their e-mails. It means loving them enough to know them, to be with them, to eat at their tables, to sleep in their beds, and to come to know their world. Until we know our suffering friends like that, we will always treat them as ideas, not as brothers and sisters.

Christ's kingdom is a global kingdom with thousands of languages rising up in songs of worship to the King. Fortunately, we have technology and easy travel to almost any destination on earth to help us in our mission to know others in this global kingdom. At Imago, we've found that knowing those who suffer is a gift that can change us deeply. How? Once we know them as friends and understand their suffering, a question surfaces. Will we act or not act in response? For kingdom people, the choice is immediately clear: to live in and practice the kingdom of God requires action.

I think you'll find, as our community has, that responding out of genuine relationship launches you into a new dimension of living, not another level of performance. Your actions may be large or small; in the kingdom they are of value, period. You may advocate against injustice and oppression in the halls of government. You may write a song that will bring awareness. You may give two coins or your whole inheritance. You may go to a community of others for a week or go as a life's work. But in every way, you are participating in the in-breaking of the kingdom in the midst of suffering.

Americans tend to assume that we know what the people in the rest of the world actually need. Genuine relationships can help set us straight on that. Once we commit to knowing others, we're likely to realize that what they say they need and what we think they need may be very different. We ought to lay down our arrogance and humbly assist them with their needs as they perceive them. They know their world, their people, and their culture. We suffer with them by letting them decide how we can best assist.

When we engage these relationships in a way that truly comes alongside to weep with those who weep, we start to taste the kingdom. We taste it in a way that is bitter and sweet at the same time. It breaks our hearts to feel what others feel daily, and it grows our hearts when we experience their reciprocal love. We are one family of kingdom people following the King. We suffer with them. That means we are brothers and sisters, not Western CEOs and third-world employees. Our relationships are familial, not contractual. Together we hurt and we feel and we love, and we are loved in return.

A redemptive quality that springs out of this kind of mutual caring is best captured by the word *solidarity*. Solidarity among brothers and sisters expresses true "with." Americans don't quite know what to make of that word except as a leftover slogan from the sixties. Maybe that's because individualism pervades our lives and our worldview so completely that we don't understand the incredible power of entering a covenant partnership with our brothers and sisters in the rest of the world.

Of course, we can't just quit being independent-minded Westerners. But sometimes a picture or two can help. Imagine the proceeds from the sale of a cow in Sudan arriving by mail at a posh Manhattan office. This actually happened after the Twin Towers had been hit on 9/11. Word of the tragedy had finally reached rural Sudan, a church that Celestin had helped establish. The church decided to respond to a faraway need in a faraway world they could barely comprehend. Their response was a gift of great value in their culture—a cow. They sold the cow for twenty dollars and sent the proceeds to an Anglican church in New York City.

I can picture some dude in an uptown Manhattan office opening an envelope from Sudan with twenty dollars inside. I wonder what he thought—if anything—before he sent it on for deposit.

Now, imagine this: a million Christians were killed in southern Sudan in only a hundred days. I remember hearing something about it on the news. Maybe you did too. Celestin was there to witness much of it.

But I did nothing in response. Did you? Honestly, it didn't even dawn on me that I should or could.

Solidarity means to suffer with. The Sudanese church expressed solidarity with those who suffered in 9/11 despite the distances in understanding and experience and miles. All of us can suffer with others in simple ways that are both profound and powerful.

Celestin told me that a man in Dallas who knew and cared for him woke up at about 3 a.m. one morning with a strong impression that he should pray and fast for his brother. He stayed up all night praying for Celestin. In the morning, he called Celestin's wife to find out what was happening. She told him that her husband was in prison again.

As Celestin told me the story, his eyes filled with tears. He saw God's care for him in waking up his friend, and he saw his friend's care in his commitment to pray—a man on the other side of the world suffering all night in prayer with the brother he loves. That is solidarity. That is suffering with. His friend's committed praying meant more to Celestin than it would have for the guy to fly to Africa and try to break him out of prison.

A second lesson we are seeing on this issue is that we are called to suffer for those who suffer.

Intentionally suffering or risking suffering seems odd at first glance. But when we see the bloodstained cross of our King, we realize that suffering is often the path to resurrection—resurrecting our hearts from the tomb of culture, sin, and the flesh.

To suffer for another can happen in a million ways, because the Spirit's creativity is boundless. Any time I commit my money, my time, my health, my opportunities, or my energy for those in need at a cost to me, I am suffering for those who suffer. My choices will speak clearly of another kingdom that is real and that has captured my heart.

My actions will preach.

"There should be less talk; a preaching point is not a meeting point," said Mother Teresa. "What do you do then? Take a broom and clean someone's house. That says enough."

Every day we tend to distance our hearts from the painful realities we see on the news. We guard our emotions so that we don't have to think about them. The reaction is understandable, but it's sick and sinful. If we stay in emotional-coma land, we will never be moved to action. We will never have the courage to suffer with those who are suffering.

But what if we wake up? What if we act?

What if, for example, we traveled on our own dime to meet some beautiful kingdom people in parts of the world that scare us? What if we gave up a chunk of our spare time to create awareness of the injustice our family members around the world are suffering? What if we cared enough to be awakened by the King late at night to pray for a brother? What if we were courageous enough to suffer with and suffer for them?

What would entering into suffering as a way to practice the presence of the kingdom of God look like in your life and mine?

It may mean that you spend your life with a people who desperately need to know the King. You educate yourself in their language and customs so you can clearly communicate His love and grace.

It may mean that you adopt a baby girl with fetal alcohol syndrome. It will be difficult at times, but you are willing to suffer with and for her. You will become a student of her uniqueness. You will show compassion, struggle with your own inadequacies, deal with the days when you lose your temper, and celebrate the small successes of your life together. Every time you look into her eyes, you will see someone for whom Jesus died.

It may mean letting go of the financial benefits that could come to you from your gifts and instead using them to advocate for or benefit another.

It may mean giving time to care for the dying.

It may mean taking a broom and cleaning someone else's mess.

The fact is, our lives do preach. But what do they preach? Do they announce to the world that God mourns with those who mourn and is risen "with healing in [His] wings"? Or do our lives announce that God is apathetic?

The church long ago ran out of time to separate the gospel from suffering in the kingdom. If we as followers of Christ choose not to live the gospel in solidarity with those who are impoverished or oppressed, then we cannot expect them to be open to receive the words of the gospel.

What if?

What if you and I started dreaming with others of ways that our lives could preach in the midst of suffering? What if we began to be more strategic about risk? What if we followed the King through many hardships to a cross?

Together we could announce resurrection. Together we would glimpse another world.

 **Voices**

Restless

There is something inside me. Something that can't wait to see you. Something that gives me butterflies and keeps me from focusing on today. Something inside me tells me to hope for things I cannot see. And so I hope because you are coming. You are coming. You've told me this and I wait in eager anticipation. There is something inside me that knows you're on your way. That same thing that knows you are coming knows everything will be different when you get here. And for that I rejoice. I sing and I dance because I know that when you come it will be true. We will finally be together and I can't seem to hope for anything else.

And so I wait. I stop and I wait. Patiently, when my feet will allow, but mostly anxiously, like a young child knowing her father will return. I move and I fuss. I pace this hardwood floor and find myself gazing out the window. I can't stand still. Soon we will be together. You've promised that you will come and because of that my song will not be silenced and my feet cannot be still.

I hear words of your arrival. Your voice whispers a promise that renews my strength. I trust you and know that you are good. And so—this waiting turns into hoping, which nourishes my love for you. Soon we will be together.

—Stefanie Faridnia

14

Slow Train Coming

Then I saw a new heaven and a new earth, for
the first heaven and the first earth had passed
away, and there was no longer any sea. I saw the
Holy City, the new Jerusalem, coming down out
of heaven from God, prepared as a bride beautifully dressed for her husband. And I heard a
loud voice from the throne saying, "Now the
dwelling of God is with men, and he will live with
them. They will be his people, and God himself
will be with them and be their God. He will wipe
every tear from their eyes. There will be no more
death or mourning or crying or pain, for the old
order of things has passed away."

Rejoice in that day and leap for joy, because
great is your reward in heaven.

We began this book with a question: What could our lives look like
if we embraced the kingdom revolution Jesus came to announce? We
asked this question in the context of both beauty and mess.

Beauty, because the presence of the kingdom is always a picture of heaven. Beauty, because to follow the teachings of Jesus our King is to find a radically new way of being human in our world. Beauty, because God's amazing story of redemption is unfolding even now—around us and in us and in spite of us—and we're invited to be part of it.

But mess too. Mess, because the ugliness of sin and sorrow and death hang like a dark cloud over the planet. Mess, because we're called to practice the presence of the kingdom in the midst of this ugliness. Mess, because what we most deeply long for is not. At least not yet.

Our kingdom quest in these pages has focused on our experience now. But in this last chapter, I want us to look into eternity and consider where the great story of God is going and what its conclusion could mean to us today.

Eternity matters because we are eternal beings who temporarily operate by the clock. Not surprisingly, eternity informed almost everything Jesus had to say about life on earth. Like us, those farmers and fishermen and housewives listening to Him by the lake were obsessed with now—with justice and healing and freedom *now.* But to help them understand their present, Jesus kept pointing them to their future.

Blessed are you *now,* Jesus said, when you endure and seek to redeem evil of all kinds because *then,* in My kingdom, your life will be beautiful and never ending. You can even leap for joy now, He said, "because great is your reward in heaven."

Do you remember what it was like when you were struggling through high school or college, looking forward to graduation? You slogged through classes, labored through homework, stayed up late to cram for exams. But sometimes your mind drifted to a picture that filled you with hope. In this picture, you're walking across the platform in cap and gown, a silly grin on your face, cameras flashing, and your hand is out to receive your diploma. All the work is behind you. All the reward is ahead.

If you are a Christ follower, heaven is the picture of your future reward. It's what will finally make sense of everything. And it's real—as real as the daily struggle is for you now. Heaven is what you can anticipate with every fiber of your being, because then all the work will be behind you, all the reward ahead. What you wouldn't give...

Heaven. It's what our lives are going to be like when we get to the end of the mess.

No doubt, there's plenty we don't and can't know about heaven, but what we *do* know is absolutely staggering. At the end of the book of Revelation, John opens a window and shows us a stunning view of the future:

> Then I saw a new heaven and a new earth, for the first heaven and the first earth had passed away, and there was no longer any sea.

Here and in the verses that follow, John gives us a preview of what eternity holds for those who want to be with God. The first thing we see is that everything is new. What is old has passed away. The earth, the sky, and all creation have been released from aging and death and brought back to perfection.

In Romans 8, Paul says that all of creation groans while it waits for this moment of newness. Groaning—that's what you did when you tossed and turned with that picture of graduation day burning in your mind's eye. If you doubted its reality for a second, you would have dumped all those chem classes. But you could see it, taste it, hear it. That's how Paul imagines every living thing feels as it longs for the future God promises.

What Paul imagined, John actually saw. His picture of heaven reveals that all our groaning and waiting will be over one day. The story of redemption will be written down to the last page.

The second thing John sees is a magnificent new city descending from God like a gift to His people. At this moment the whole history of God's people will culminate. Where in the past God's presence had dwelled in the temple at Jerusalem and in our hearts by His Spirit, now the new, eternal Jerusalem has arrived to become God's home—and ours with Him:

> Now the dwelling of God is with men, and he will live with
> them. They will be his people, and God himself will be with
> them and be their God. He will wipe every tear from their eyes.
> There will be no more death or mourning or crying or pain, for
> the old order of things has passed away.

I can't think of any social or political visionary who has painted such a sweeping and compelling portrait of a world made right. Deep in our hearts, we *know* it's right. We recognize heaven as the place we've always been homesick for. Do you know that unnameable longing? I do. The psalmist describes it like this:

> One thing I ask of the LORD,
>   this is what I seek,
> that I may dwell in the house of the LORD
>   all the days of my life,
> to gaze upon the beauty of the LORD
>   and to seek him in his temple.

But the day will come when that one thing our souls desire will be granted. We won't be homesick anymore. One day, we'll be walking and talking in the house of God, fully alive in the shining presence of our King.

Since our real future is so amazing and wonderful, I find it odd that followers of Jesus think so little about it.

Maybe we're too focused on the stress and strain of the now to think ahead. Or maybe we assume that heaven will be so completely different from our daily experience that we don't know what to think of it. So we don't.

Why not change that? A closer look at what the Bible says about heaven can set us free to think differently, better, and more about our future. I recommend Randy Alcorn's thorough study titled simply *Heaven*. He lists commonly held assumptions about heaven among Christ followers, and then he compares those with what the Bible says. For example, we assume that heaven is a completely nonphysical experience. We'll float around in something like ether there and morph from place to place (think "Beam me up, Scotty").

But the Bible shows that heaven will be a restored physical world. Imagine an earth that had never fallen under the curse of sin and death. Imagine a natural order with all the beauty we see now but with none of the destruction, threat, or limits. (Revelation 22, for example, talks about fruit trees that bear every month, not just once a year.)

- We assume that heaven will feel unfamiliar and otherworldly. But the Bible describes a flourishing realm of city and nature, of people and conversations, of streets to walk down and good food to be enjoyed. Christ talks about heaven as the place that's prepared for us and welcoming and familiar, a place we would choose to be over all others, a place that will give us that ultimate "Home at last!" feeling.

- We assume that in heaven people will be spirits (nice ghosts, though, like Casper), not embodied as we are now. But the Bible tells us that we will exist in eternity in a body that has been "raised in glory"—a physical body similar to the resurrected Jesus—that will never again wrestle with sickness, want, pain, or aging.

- We assume that in heaven we'll be without our favorite things. If you're a six-year-old, that would mean no pandas or puppies. If you're an adult, that would mean you should brace for a sterile environment (think hospital waiting room, people shuffling around in white gowns, nothing decent to read). But the Bible shows pictures of the lion and the lamb lying down together. The restored natural world of heaven is alive with life and harmony, with richness and play.

- We think of heaven as static. Harps and clouds and very long sing-alongs. Nothing changes. You're in a huge cathedral singing "Hallelujah!" at the top of your lungs, and the song…just…never…ends. No use looking at your watch and edging toward the door. You're going to be here for a while. But the Bible describes a heaven that is neither static nor boring. Instead, it is a dynamic, vibrant reality. You will have things to do, people to visit, meaningful relationships, fulfilling responsibilities. You will finally be able to experience as much of the joy of living and learning as you've so far just imagined.

- We tend to imagine a heaven where we will have no desire because everything will already be perfect. But the Bible shows us that we have been created in the image of God to be passionate about many things, to pursue, to enjoy, and to achieve. What we are most profoundly created to pursue with passion is God. We're created in His image; we're created for intimacy with Him. On earth we spend a lot of energy pursuing deceptive substitutes. But in heaven we will enjoy the physical presence of God, and our desire for Him will be continually fulfilled, renewed, and expanded.

As we let the truth about heaven push aside our wrong assumptions, we'll find ourselves wanting heaven more and being defeated by earth less. We'll begin to understand that thinking truthfully about our future isn't optional for kingdom revolutionaries; it's required. It radically changes how we feel, what we want, and what we decide. Jesus is our example on this. In Hebrews we read that Jesus "for the joy set before him endured the cross, scorning its shame."

The sheer joy of keeping a clear picture of our future in God releases us to wholeheartedly embrace His kingdom agenda now. We can enter into poverty and hunger with joy. We can take the lesser seat with serenity. We can say no to lust and greed in the upside-down kingdom of earth that exalts those very sins. We can understand the blessing of weeping with those who weep. We can sacrifice our creativity and our opportunities to press for justice and creation care—and sense the hope in our sacrifice. We can devote our lives to spreading the wonderful news of salvation in Jesus Christ. We can risk rejection, discomfort, and exclusion for the joy of knowing the truth about our future.

I invite you to join me in keeping a true picture of heaven on the wall of our hearts. Our future is beautiful and true, and we can anticipate it with wild hope.

If a picture of the perfect world still feels too overwhelming or vague for you, John presents another visual moment that could be your picture of heaven. He pictures the New Jerusalem "coming down out of heaven from God, prepared as a bride beautifully dressed for her husband."

You know the feeling you have when you're at a wedding, listening to the music, waiting for the ceremony to start? Remember the anticipation, the intense emotion, the richness of meaning in the event? Then the groom and the groomsmen enter up front. From the back, a procession starts down the aisle, from flower girls to bridesmaids. Suddenly the music swells, everyone stands and turns, the doors burst open, and in sweeps the lovely bride on her father's arm. Everyone is in awe of the beauty and power of the moment. You know you're all about to witness a new beginning that was always meant to be.

Keep that picture of heaven in your mind too. There's a wedding in the future, and it is ours. We wait in great anticipation for God and His people to finally be united. We wait and ache for the pleasure of what is about to happen.

And it will.

One day, the gates of heaven will burst open, and people of the kingdom will be together forever with our King at last.

For now we wait, and waiting is hard work. Hope can wear thin and slide into discouragement.

When God, who says He is good, refuses to step in and end the mess, discouragement can turn to doubt or anger. If God is good, why are people living on the streets? If God is good, why did my child die of cancer? If God is good, why…? Our list of frustrations and disappointments can go on and on. Before long, we look at the mess around us and decide we're going to use it to accuse God of having a flawed character, of breaking His word.

But the New Testament presents another answer. Not the one we want, which is for God to snap His fingers and make the mess go away. Instead, the Bible shows us a God who chooses to enter personally into the mess. "I will come down and go into the mess with you," Jesus announces with His words and life. "If you suffer, I will suffer in your place. If death is what stings, then I will die in your place and defeat death. If sin is what has ruined the earth and humanity, then I will be the sinless sacrifice to restore, redeem, and reclaim."

That is the salvation message of the New Testament—amazing grace, forgiveness for what we could not in ourselves overcome, hope in darkness, life when we had lost hope in life.

But there is also the kingdom message of the New Testament. It is this: where Christ entered, suffered, and died to bring life, you and I are invited to do the same for others in His name. You and I—not some spiritual superheroes of our imagination—are invited to embrace the vision of Jesus and enter into our own world as His representatives.

Do you remember Bob Dylan's first gospel album? The cover of *Slow Train Coming* shows workers laying down track ahead of a train that is already steaming into sight. The man in the foreground holds a cross-shaped pick high over his shoulder. But his eye is trained on the rail bed at his feet. He can hear the train. He can feel it coming. There is work to do, and it cannot wait.

"There's a slow, slow train comin' up around the bend," Dylan sang. "Like a thief in the night, He'll replace wrong with right when he returns."

This is our true story—the story of God, a King who is arriving in different ways in our world every day, but who one day will come in complete and unending fullness with redemption for those who love Him and judgment for those who don't. The apostle John wrote, "We know that when he appears, we shall be like him, for we shall see him as he is. Everyone who has this hope in him purifies himself."

Can you see heaven approaching?

Can you hear it?

Every day under our feet, creation groans and trembles with its approach. And we have a kingdom to embrace and a King to worship.

Appendix

The Gospel and the Kingdom

Sometimes it seems as though we find two gospels in the New Testament: the gospel of Jesus and the gospel about Jesus. The gospel *of* Jesus is usually taken to mean His announcement of the kingdom and the life He embodied in His loving actions toward the world. The gospel *about* Jesus refers to His atoning work on the cross and His resurrection, through which we can receive the forgiveness of sin through our faith and repentance. The two gospels even correlate to a schism in the church, with more liberal churches living the gospel of Jesus, doing the good deeds of the kingdom, while more conservative churches preach the gospel about Jesus, focusing on the personal salvation He offers to those who put their faith in Him.

I believe, however, that the two are actually one gospel. When we lose the tension that comes from holding both together, we experience an unhealthy and unbiblical pendulum swing in our faith.

If all we value is the salvation gospel, we tend to miss the rest of Christ's message. Taken out of the context of the kingdom, the call to faith in Christ gets reduced to something less than the New Testament teaches. The reverse is also true. If we value a kingdom gospel at the expense of the liberating message of the Cross and the empty tomb and a call to repentance, we miss a central tenet of kingdom life. Without faith in Jesus, there is no transferring of our lives into the new world of the kingdom.

This dichotomy, however, doesn't fully describe how we may or may not participate in what God is doing on earth. People don't stand outside the doorway of the kingdom, waiting to get through the salvation gate in order to enter and experience kingdom realities. Rather people are tasting, touching, and embracing pieces of the kingdom all the time. The love of creation, for example, is experienced by those who follow Christ and those who do not. The invitation to embrace the kingdom then becomes an opportunity for us to get side by side with those who don't know Jesus but are attracted to His creation and to point out to them that what they love is compelling evidence that they were made for another world that is accessible through faith in Christ.

In this way, their participation in the kingdom becomes a point where the gospel can be more fully articulated. If we're participating along with them, followers of Christ get to explain to them both the worldview of the kingdom and the salvation our King offers. They get to encounter Christ without having to find a way through the sterile walls of religion in search of Him.

Therefore participation in the kingdom life by those who follow Jesus becomes an opportunity to serve the Great Commission in a much fuller way. Our joyful announcing of the reign of God through His in-breaking kingdom becomes a beginning point of gospel proclamation.

To the degree that conservative churches abandon the tactile expression of God's reign to the least in our communities, they compromise their ability to proclaim a viable Savior to a suffering world. At least the culture around us listens less because what is being said about Jesus is not being lived out in the mess of their lives. Christians are simply saying that Jesus is King without also living out His reign in the streets.

On the more liberal side, churches may champion the good deeds done as kingdom expressions but leave out the unique and exclusive claims of Christ as the only way to God. One result of this scenario is that Christ followers demonstrate convincing redemptive work in a community that, unfortunately, rarely leads to the personal redemption Jesus promised.

Both scenarios present an incomplete gospel.

When we personally and holistically embody both gospels under Christ's kingdom reign, we are able to proclaim the good news of Jesus in a profound way. The cross of Christ and the empty tomb bring forth the power to give new life to individuals and to restore creation. It is not one or the other. The New Testament shows us a God who is restoring humanity as part of His restoring of the world.

At Imago Dei, we see many people putting their faith in Jesus in the context of the kingdom. But the temptation to reduce the message of Jesus is never far away. We are sometimes tempted to let go of the tension and either practice a religion of good deeds or preach personal salvation in Christ. Better to hold on to the tension and to view it as God's invitation to collaborate together with the Spirit in putting forth a whole gospel to our city and world.

We see the great beauty of people knowing that they are forgiven of their sins and accepted as God's children through the grace of Jesus. More often than not, though, we see it happen after they have felt and experienced the goodness of the kingdom break into their lives through the good deeds of kingdom people who care enough to serve them *and* who care enough to tell them about Jesus' sacrificial love. It's through this kind of kingdom living that both the gospel and the kingdom are united to bring another world to bear upon our society and our souls, thus creating the new humanity that God predestined us to be and become.

Appendix

2

Kingdom Shifts

I hope this book is calling you to make some very practical changes. Toward that end, I want to describe several important shifts we've seen our faith community and the churches we work with go through while following Christ on this kingdom journey. These shifts in both thought and action strike us as crucial for the journey ahead.

FROM COMING TO GOING

We live in an entertainment culture, and we love to go to entertaining events. The church gets that and has taken it to heart. Attracting people to come to us is not the worst thing, for sure. But Jesus didn't use that model. He went to the people. Yet, in our current culture, churches work to reach those who are not yet Christ followers by attracting them through programs and entertaining services that appeal to them. Full-service churches cover the suburban landscape, usually bringing with them a gospel of happiness through the medium of entertainment. Of course, bringing the people who don't know Jesus to church is a good thing. But seeing the people who don't know Jesus come to faith is a miracle. Unfortunately, our calling to make disciples is often at odds with an approach that is primarily structured to get people in the door of the church, an approach that keeps us from going to the people as Jesus modeled.

The shift that's needed, I propose, is for kingdom people to become the sent people of God, to shift from coming to going. The theological mandate described in Matthew 28:18–20 reveals just a small piece of the sending nature of God. Beginning in Genesis 3, God went looking for fallen Adam. Throughout the Old Testament, God sent deliverers, judges, kings, and prophets to His people with the promise that He would be sending the Messiah. Jesus called forth His disciples and sent them to announce the kingdom. Once the Son rejoined the Father after His ascension, God sent the Spirit.

Now, Father, Son, and Spirit send the church into the world to proclaim the crucified and risen Christ with word and deed.

I see two reasons kingdom people should reclaim this sending posture.

First, in order to truly make disciples, we must bring kingdom people to a place where they are living out their sent identity as missionaries to the culture. I don't mean only vocational missionaries who raise support and work for organizations. I mean every believer. Think about it. If we believe that our highest task is to bring someone to an entertaining event, we handicap our formation as disciples and missionaries.

Second, in a culture where suspicion of the church is endemic, the world must see the gospel lived out beyond the walls of the church or it probably won't see it all. There is realness and appeal to the gospel when it is on display in the lives of unpaid believers *outside of* any church agenda or program. A Jesus encountered off a platform and away from a program or building reveals Himself to be not so much a pop icon as lover, healer, and truth teller to people in need.

That identity is also who we are and what we are called to be. The main reason people of the King gather is to worship the One who sends us back into the culture to be His hands and feet and voice to others.

The implications for pastors and leaders of this shift in focus are many. To name a few:

- We need to educate the church as to its sent identity as the people of God.
- We need to repent of building our own empires so that churches become a mission unto themselves.
- We need to empower people for the unique expression of mission that their gifting gives them.
- We need, in other words, to learn how to pastor all believers as missionaries and equip and train their hearts and minds for their task.

What I'm talking about will have monumental implications on areas like staffing and structure. Yet I believe these shifts and others like them will express the faithful response the church must make to live out the mission of Jesus in our time and place.

FROM PRAGMATIC HOW-TO TO PASSIONATE WANT-TO

One of the assumptions we often make is that Christians want to live out the mission of God but don't know how. On the basis of Scripture, however, we'd have to question that assumption.

Actually, people who were touched by Jesus had very little information on how to share their faith, yet they were effective witnesses. Mostly what they had was a deep desire. For this reason, another shift I recommend is a move from pragmatism to passion.

This would begin with honest repentance for our sins of omission. After all, Jesus began His ministry with the call to repentance. The idea of this word is simply to turn around. The turning is not for individuals only, it's not a once-for-all event, and it's not only for sins of commission. Rather, repentance becomes the gift that God gives us and our communities so that we may find forgiveness from sin and continual renewal in our hearts for God and His gospel.

Another faulty assumption is that all believers desire to share their faith, love their neighbors, and see the world won to Christ. In a weird way, the church has embraced an ethical humanism when it comes to mission. We simply tend to think that everyone is good-hearted about it and would do it if they knew how. Hence the outpouring of how-to titles for everything from church marketing to personal prayer life.

What intrigues me about our embracing of this phenomenon is the purposeful lack of how-tos in the New Testament, either from Jesus to His disciples or from God to the church. What we need is to be captured by the want-to of God.

The leadership implications of this line of thinking are many, but allow me to suggest a few:

- We must give a clear picture of the love of God.
- We must rescue the idea of mission from the guilt task that it has become so people can be captured by the love of God.
- Leaders need to teach clearly that if we love God, we will always express it in our love for others. Too often people are so caught up with God that they have no time for people, but to this we must bring correction and rebuke. The love of God makes me a lover of all people or my love is simply a false religion.

We are not failing for lack of programs and pragmatism but for lack of desire. If we can honestly confront the fact that we don't desire to love the world as God does, then we can begin the process of being transformed by the gospel ourselves. When we go through this shift, I believe God will move in tremendous power through His people and His church to display His love to the world.

FROM PROTECTION TO PROCLAMATION

Followers of Jesus have often responded to the eroding morality of society by retreating into protectionism. We have created a parallel culture—a safe haven from the world around us—but in doing this, we've lost touch with the people near us. For the same reason, the church has lost its voice in the public square.

Consider, for example, the issue of homosexual marriage. Most evangelicals believe the Bible teaches that homosexuality is wrong. Yet while the church is defending heterosexual marriage, it is not addressing the issue of divorce very well—an issue that is as much a problem inside the church as outside. One outcome of politicizing our beliefs is that the church is now seen in partisan terms—either conservative right or liberal left. Both associations make it very difficult to speak of Jesus as the world's King. *King of which party?* our listeners might wonder. In Portland, where an open and affirming stance toward gender orientation is the norm, we've found that when we talk to people about Jesus, simply calling ourselves Christians often leads the conversation *away* from Christ and into politics.

The gospel clearly indicates that if we change someone's morality without changing his or her heart through faith in Christ, we have not done anything of eternal significance. So when church-based efforts on these issues cut us off from sharing the life-changing message of Jesus, our mission in the world takes a double hit.

Christian protectionism is at work when we have our own music,

T-shirts, clubs, and weight-loss programs. There's nothing wrong with these ventures in themselves, but what does the world see when we do this? Does it see in us a radical new humanity living out the life of Jesus in relationship with broken and sinful people, or does it see powerful financial and political interests profiting from a clearly defined consumer base?

What, then, might be required for the people of the kingdom to make a shift from protection to proclamation?

For one thing, we will need to reexamine how Christ has called us to interact with the world. The gospel calls us to live as aliens and strangers in the world. Yet I don't see this call requiring that we legislate our moral differences as much as proclaim our love for Jesus and the love He has given us for the world.

Some may disagree and say, for example, that the motive behind the Defense of Marriage Act is a love for God. I don't doubt that, yet I'd ask, Does your love for God move you to love others with *an expression of love they can understand and experience*? If the answer is probably not, then we're moving further away from our most important value, not closer.

I believe we must choose to be proclaimers of God's love over being protectors of morality. The proclamation of the gospel is much larger than simply explaining the issues of atonement and personal faith in Jesus. To be sure, the church stands on a tightrope between religious morality and a broken culture. It is messy business to walk on this tightrope. Yet that is where we are to be. As Christ's followers, we must care as much about the sins of omission as we do the sins of commission. Our failure to love the world is *our* sin to own.

Owning it, it seems to me, will require repentance as a first step. But that step will create solidarity between us and other sinful people who don't know Christ, because it demonstrates that we are both radically dependent on the grace of God. No longer can we stand with the protective posture of us versus them. Instead, we will find ourselves creating pathways for people to Christ. We will become a church that puts itself at risk in order to love like Jesus.

As part of this move, the church will need to equip God's people with the relational tools to engage in dialogue with those who hold opposing viewpoints. We must let the love of God lead us in this area, but I doubt we'd be sending people out to win debates about creation versus evolution. More likely, we'd be sending them into the world with the tools to present God as the attractive being that He is, sending them out not to win souls but to proclaim Jesus in word and deed, not to make their churches bigger but to live out their faith in an authentic way among their neighbors.

The move from protection to proclamation will also require us to understand the culture in which we live. This may be the biggest stretch for many of us, because *discipleship* has tended to focus on matters of being part of the church while *mission* has been left to those going overseas. We will need to go out and begin relationships with the people and places around us, to engage the culture for the sake of Christ. There's no one right way of doing this. Each setting is different and has its own specific needs and assumptions that will affect how we proclaim Christ.

The changes will take time, but I believe they are the only way to get back on mission. Leaders who model a proclamation lifestyle will have enormous influence on moving others to engage in their missional task of living as proclaimers of Christ to the world.

From Rational to Holistic

It is no longer safe to assume that we can introduce the gospel to people through the pure means of reason. The reality is, in a pluralistic culture, people are happy to live with an illogical worldview and embrace competing truths without feeling much dissonance. So we have to shift from being people who primarily address the issues of the mind/will and become people who can minister the gospel to the whole person— physical, emotional, relational, and spiritual. In doing so, we may find that the heart has been ignored the most, and it is the faculty most in need of the gospel.

In 1974, a group of people including John Stott, the great Western theologian, and C. René Padilla, Stott's counterpart in Latin America, drafted the Lausanne Covenant. In it they lay out a doctrinal statement that explains the gospel in a holistic way. This document has served over the years to give missionaries a much-needed doctrinal compass with which to live the gospel in different cultures. The covenant lays out with balance and biblical faithfulness a picture of a holistic gospel. I would summarize its message as "the whole gospel to the whole person and the whole world."

At some point in the history of the American church, our gospel seems to have become fragmented—cut off from the whole person— and, not surprisingly, smaller. But in order to enter our kingdom voca- tion, we must preach the exclusivity of Christ and the life-changing message of Jesus while at the same time putting that love on physical display through, for example, social action.

In postmodernity, experience has become the litmus test for what is true. The church has tended to be scared of this approach, believing that it somehow undermines the authority of the Bible. I understand the con- cern, but I believe it's overstated and misleading. Rather, I see the desire for experience as a healthy reaction to rationalism. In the church, this calls us to realize that while Jesus claimed to be the Truth, He is not a rational proposition. Christ's life is a physical proclamation of the love of God—full of risk, sacrifice, and rejection—so the world may know that

God is real and loves the world. He is the divine Son of God, who is to be known and experienced and obeyed as the world's King.

Now we are called to follow in His same life, taking the whole gospel to the whole person.

FROM RELEVANCE TO INFLUENCE

If the culture is to be shaped by the people of the King, then our relevance must be leveraged to influence the culture for the sake of the kingdom. In doing so, we will regain a voice in all areas of culture as we use our gifts and influence to shape the landscape of the world.

To be sure, finding a voice in the culture means we must speak the language the culture understands. In recent decades the church has made relevance a primary work in communicating the gospel. But relevance is merely a starting point in our relationship to culture, not its destination.

If you went to a tribal people who were still practicing cannibalism, you would hardly throw a party at which you invited others to join you in eating your neighbor. Overlaying the value of relevance would be the greater value of influence. How do you get the cannibals to stop eating one another? That would be influencing change in the culture. We know that the gospel has the power to not simply transform lives but culture as well.

Unfortunately, our attempts at influencing culture have been hindered by the protectionist mind-set I mentioned earlier, often pushing the church back into irrelevance. One remedy: the church can have real influence in our times if we see our whole life in relationship with God. For example, our skills and gifts aren't meant to be utilized only inside the church but to shape the world with kingdom life.

I know businessmen who do small tasks for the church while they spend sixty-plus hours a week in the marketplace. Seldom do their jobs and their faith intersect, and when they do, it is mostly in the area of evangelism or benevolence. But what if they were discipled in such a way that they understood their vocation as their expression of the gospel in the culture where they can serve as an agent of influence for the kingdom? The ramifications would be enormous.

Practically, it might look like this:

- A CEO begins to create a culture that reflects the kingdom in her workplace. This may be as simple as requiring employees to enter community service or as complex as instituting initiatives within the workplace that address employee needs such as financial counseling, day care, and others.

- An entrepreneur leverages his business for a different bottom line than the dollar and moves his company to create jobs for young people with criminal records while mentoring them in areas of life responsibility.

- An artist creates excellent, well-respected art, and through his work he is able to communicate themes of redemption. The artist trains young people to apply their skills for the same ends but with applications that are unique to each individual. The act of a creator intentionally expressing the nature of his Creator becomes a bridge to the gospel.

In sum, we need to redefine what an influential church looks like in our culture. Most of us envision an influential church as large and exceptionally resourced. But influence can happen with any church, regardless of size. The way it happens is simply by discipling people to be on mission as influencers of the culture. The pastor's role in this shift would be to shepherd—come alongside and help followers of the King re-vision their lives in the ways I've described.

The dream I have for the church is that as it enters the mission field of the United States, it will one day equip and send people into the culture who are respected for their relevant lives and who are effecting ideas that are shaping our world.

This is the gospel outcome as seen in the Abrahamic blessing of Genesis: God's new humanity will be a blessing to all people as we live faithfully in the love of God and offer ourselves holistically to the mission for which He called us.

Excursions into the Kingdom: A Guide for Conversation

Part One: Discovering the Kingdom

Chapter 1: Beautiful, Mess

1. Where have you experienced the mess in your story?
2. Can you imagine the possibility that Jesus could bring beauty from that place? What might that beauty look like to you?
3. Where have you experienced beauty in your story?
4. What response do you have to Rick's invitation to "get out of religion free"? Did you feel fear, joy, confusion, or something else? Talk about it.

Chapter 2: What If?

1. What are your primary obstacles in understanding Jesus as King of His kingdom in the here and now?
2. If you look into your own life, can you see glimpses of His kingdom breaking in? If so, where?
3. Would you say your experience as a Christian thus far is more like a consuming, mysterious adventure or a set of rules that accompany salvation insurance?

Chapter 3: Harpooning God

1. Rick describes how we can attempt to control God. Have you ever tried to "put Jesus into service"? Tried to get God to "endorse [your] agenda"? Tried to "get God back on track" in your life? If so, describe what happened.

2. Did you come away from that experience thinking or living differently? Would you say you're still caught up in these or similar futile attempts?

3. What teaching or dimension of Jesus' gospel of the kingdom seem most at odds to your need for a "useful" God?

4. Where do you see "King-less errors" creeping into popular Christian products, lyrics, or slogans?

PART TWO: RE-VISIONING LIFE IN THE KINGDOM

Chapter 4: Seeing Through

1. The kingdom is near, so near, yet so hard to see sometimes. Where have you seen the kingdom breaking through recently?

2. How do you understand repentance as an event? as a practice?

3. What is the connection between repentance and our ability to see the kingdom?

4. Reread the end of the chapter, from "Do we actually want the revolution of Jesus to break into our lives and our community?" to the end. What fear or worry might be holding you back from surrendering to the kingdom of Jesus?

5. What might be some needs in your community you believe Jesus would care deeply about? Ask yourself why you don't and where you could start to make a change. Talk about it in your "borrowed basement" group.

Chapter 5: A Dimension of Being

1. In what ways are you prone to next-level thinking in your faith? How does that kind of thinking put you at odds with how God actually works in the world?

2. What do you love about *being* rather than *doing*? What do you most resist or dislike about it?

3. Rick writes, "Choosing to live in the kingdom dimension creates some major shifts in our thinking." How might your life change if you shifted from advancing to embracing? from producing to growing?

4. Would you rather build something for Jesus or participate with Him in what He is growing? Be honest. Can you articulate the reason for your answer?

Chapter 6: Jesus' Kingdom of Peace

1. What circumstances are most likely to cause you *dis*harmony in your world?

2. Do you believe, based on your experience, that God can use even broken notes to make His song beautiful? Talk about it.

3. Joseph lived through many years of suffering and exile before he could say to the brothers who had betrayed him, "What you meant for evil God meant for good." Can you relate? If so, talk about it.

4. What might be keeping you from trusting that God is always at work in your life to bring harmony and beauty from disharmony and brokenness? What insight might the biblical stories of Joseph or Jesus have for you today?

Chapter 7: Already, Not Yet

1. How have you witnessed the reality that opposing forces are competing with God for the same turf in our world?

2. Rick writes about the need to hold on to the both/and truth of the "already and not yet" kingdom. Talk about that tension in your own experience or in the experience of your church.

3. In what ways does living in the not yet bring you comfort? In what ways does it bring you disappointment and hurt?

4. Rick writes about God's "amazing judo move" that He uses to attack the kingdom of darkness. What is it? If you've seen it at work in your life, talk about it.

PART THREE: PRACTICING THE PRESENCE OF THE KINGDOM

Chapter 8: Signposts of Heaven

1. This chapter is full of imagery that helps to capture the teachings of the kingdom: light, signposts, salt, sent ones. Pick one that could help you today to both rest and act in the deep reality of the kingdom.

2. Think about Joe down at the corner of Sixth and Pine with his camp stove, making meals for passersby. What inspires you about that example of kingdom living? What scares you about it?

3. Identify a couple of places of pressing need in your community. What might the kingdom look like if it broke in there?

4. What obstacles keep you and those you know from being signposts of heaven in your community? How could you begin to clear away those obstacles?

Chapter 9: Sharing the News About Our King

1. Talking to others about our faith just might be the most difficult spiritual practice for followers of Christ. How would you describe your feelings about this undertaking?

2. How was Jesus first presented to you? As a simple, quick *decision* to believe that would bring immediate payoffs? Or as a *person* who would reshape you from the inside out over the course of a long journey?

3. Rick describes the Jesus way as narrow, a long walk, a dirt path, all about endurance, and more often marked by solitude than a crowd. Do you agree? If so, why?

4. Rick writes, "People on the Jesus way, living by the Jesus truth in the Jesus life, see their whole lives through the rearview mirror of grace." What does this statement mean to you? How could it inform how you introduce Jesus to others?

Chapter 10: Welcome the Child

1. What kinds of attitudes or values would you need to lay aside in order to come to Jesus as a child?

2. If you don't live with children, how could you create an intentional connection with a child or children so that you can learn kingdom living from them? Where could you give your time that would allow that kind of connection to flourish?

3. How will it affect our relationship with Jesus and others if we refuse to become like children before our King?

4. How could the kingdom break into your community where kids are in the most need? How could you be a part of that?

Chapter 11: Alive in a Million Mysteries

1. Rick describes creation as "the place where we strive to receive and to steward, not simply consume." How could you and your church community apply this statement in redemptive ways?

2. Would you agree with Tim that clearing out a mess of blackberry vines that had overtaken a hillside "is the gospel"? Discuss.

3. "Without a doubt, creation *is* scarred by sin," writes Rick. But "our attitudes about it are scarred too." What evidence do you see for both statements in the world today?

4. What could it look like if you and/or your church practiced the kingdom by creating or restoring sacred spaces in your community or in a community you have access to?

Chapter 12: Stamp of Empire

1. With Rick's argument early in this chapter in mind, would you say you have over- or underestimated the power of money during the last year?

2. When you look at the way you give, share, and care, to what empire are you declaring allegiance?

3. Why are our finances often one of the last places we let the King rule in our lives?

4. Rick ends this chapter by saying that money is put in our care with the word *Love* written across it, which leads him to arrive at a defining question: *Who will I love with that dollar, and how?* Talk about how this approach to your resources—even your discretionary cash—could change your week.

Chapter 13: We Must Go Through Many Hardships

1. Everyone suffers, but suffering for the gospel is different. How?

2. Share your reaction to Rick's statement, "my freedoms shape my expectation, and my expectation is simple and powerful: suffering is to be avoided at all costs."

3. What role does accepting suffering as an *intentional lifestyle* have in spreading the gospel of the kingdom? For example, what might choosing to suffer accomplish that nothing else could?

4. In what ways might a fear of suffering have prevented you from participating in His kingdom?

5. What places could you go or what circumstances could you be in to listen, give comfort, and proclaim the love of the King to those who suffer?

Chapter 14: Slow Train Coming

1. "Heaven. It's what our lives are going to be like when we get to the end of the mess," writes Rick. What do you most long for in eternity? Why?

2. How might you embrace kingdom living more fully if you had a more complete understanding of heaven?

3. "We wait in great anticipation for God and His people to finally be united," writes Rick. "We wait and ache for the pleasure of what is about to happen." What counsel would you give to a beloved fellow believer who doesn't see much benefit to living in hope of heaven?

Acknowledgments

First, I want to thank my amazing tribe, the great people at Imago Dei Community. Thank you for being courageous enough to seek the kingdom in authentic ways and for giving your lives for another world. The journey has just begun. Thanks to my incredible staff and elders for putting up with the crazy ideas I've tried to express in this book and for being bold enough to spend their lives on them. Thanks to Jeff and Eric for standing in the thick of it day in and day out. Who would have thought so many years ago that God was bringing us together for this? Special thanks to my great friend Don Miller—may God continue to use your gifts for His glory. And sincere thanks to the poets and writers from Imago Dei who gave me permission to include their works as expressions of a growing kingdom awareness among us: Monique Amado, Nathan Bubna, Jan Carson, Stefanie Faridnia, Sabrina Fountain, Caleb Kytonen, Vania Moore, Kristin Mulhern Noblin, and Raeben Nolan.

More thanks to: Clint Kemp, I'm grateful for friendship, cigars, and sacred-space moments that make life a bit more clear. The La Mesa family for being a global community seeking the kingdom together. Chris Seay for the casa and friendship. Eric Knox for being in the mess with me. David Nicholas—who has since passed away—for giving me a shot at church planting and for cheering us on. Dave Smith for always believing in me, even when there was not much to believe in. Ron Frost and Gerry Breshears for helping me think about God. Haddon Robinson for your teaching and your wisdom. Gabe Lyons and all the great people at Relevate.

Thanks to my editor and writing coach, David Kopp, who, when time was short, worked from my chapter drafts and other materials to help me craft something we can both celebrate. Without you, this book never would have happened. To all the other good people at WaterBrook Multnomah who have contributed so much, thank you.

I want to acknowledge several authors who have greatly influenced my thinking: Dallas Willard, C. René Padilla, and George Eldon Ladd. Eugene Peterson taught me how to be a pastor. Thanks also to Sixpence None the Richer, whose lyrics made me think and feel and whose album, also titled *This Beautiful Mess,* started my mind moving down this road.

I especially want to thank my family: my kids Josh, Kaylee, Zach, and Bryce for just being who God is calling you to be. May you continue to taste and see that He is good and that His kingdom reigns forever. Thank you, Jeanne, for putting up with the craziness for the last twenty-four years; it's gone so fast, and you've made it a beautiful journey. Thanks to Mom, Dad, Kellie, and Mike; my parents-in-law, Darrell and Suzi; and the rest of our family for all the love and support.

Finally, thanks to my friend Paul. Without you and Diane, we never would have taken the leap of faith to start Imago.

Notes

SCRIPTURE REFERENCES

Foreword
He will set the captives free: see Isaiah 61:1

Part One: Discovering the Kingdom
The kingdom of God is near: Mark 1:15; Luke 10:9, 11; 21:31
The kingdom of God is within you: Luke 17:21

Chapter 1: Beautiful, Mess
Blessed are the poor in spirit: Matthew 5:3

Chapter 2: What If?
The kingdom of heaven is like treasure: Matthew 13:44
The kingdom of heaven is like yeast: Matthew 13:33
The kingdom of heaven is like a mustard seed: Matthew 13:31–32
The kingdom of heaven: Matthew 3:2; 4:17; 5:3, 10, 19, 20; 7:21;
      8:11; 10:7; 11:11, 12; 13:11, 24, 31, 33, 44, 45, 47, 52; 16:19;
      18:1, 3, 4, 23; 19:12, 14, 23; 20:1; 22:2, 23:13; 25:1
The kingdom of God: Matthew 12:28; 19:24; 21:31, 43; Mark 1:15;
      4:11, 26, 30; 9:1, 47; 10:14, 15, 23, 24, 25; 12:34; 14:25; 15:43;
      Luke 4:43; 6:20; 7:28; 8:1, 10; 9:2, 11, 27, 60, 62; 10:9, 11; 11:20;

13:18, 20, 28, 29; 14:15; 16:16; 17:20, 21; 18:16, 17, 24, 25, 29;
19:11; 21:31; 22:16, 18; 23:51; John 3:3, 5; Acts 1:3; 8:12; 14:22;
19:8; 28:23, 31; Romans 14:17; 1 Corinthians 4:20; 6:9, 10; 15:50;
Galatians 5:21; Colossians 4:11; 2 Thessalonians 1:5

Chapter 3: Harpooning God

Jesus traveled about: Luke 8:1

The kingdom of God is at hand: Mark 1:15, NASB

The kingdom of God is within you: Luke 17:21

The kingdom coming on the clouds at the end of time:
    see Matthew 26:64; Mark 14:62

In this world you will have trouble: John 16:33

Christ in you, the hope of glory: Colossians 1:27

Chapter 4: Seeing Through

Jesus went into Galilee: Mark 1:14–15

The kingdom of God is near: Mark 1:15

The kingdom of God is at hand: Mark 1:15, NASB

Clap your hands: Psalm 47:1–4

Say among the nations: Psalm 96:10–13

Shout and be glad: Zechariah 2:10–11

Repent: Mark 1:15

Seek first his kingdom and his righteousness:
    Matthew 6:33

Chapter 5: A Dimension of Being

He told them another parable: Matthew 13:31–33

Key verse in Colossians: Colossians 1:13

Though it is the smallest of all your seeds: Matthew 13:32

The kingdom of heaven is like yeast: Matthew 13:33

Chapter 6: Jesus' Kingdom of Peace

Glory to God in the highest: Luke 2:14

For the good of those who love him: Romans 8:28

You intended to harm me, but God intended it for good: Genesis 50:20

There will be no more death or mourning or crying or pain:
Revelation 21:4–5

Chapter 7: Already, Not Yet

Jesus told them another parable: Matthew 13:24–26

A farmer went out to sow his seed: Matthew 13:3

The kingdom of heaven is like a man who sowed good seed: Matthew
13:24–30

The good seed stands for the sons of the kingdom: Matthew 13:38

At the end of the age: Matthew 13:40–41

The righteous will shine like the sun: Matthew 13:43

He causes all things to work for good: see Romans 8:28

Chapter 8: Signposts of Heaven

You are the light of the world: Matthew 5:14–16

As you go, preach this message: Matthew 10:7–8

Go into all the world: Mark 16:15

I am the way and the truth and the life: John 14:6

Anyone who has seen me has seen the Father: John 14:9

As the Father has sent me, I am sending you: John 20:21

But God wanted them to go into all the world: see Mark 16:15

He came to seek and to save: see Luke 19:10

Chapter 9: Sharing the News About Our King

The Spirit of the Lord is on me: Luke 4:18

These people are like trees planted by a flowing stream: see Psalm 1:3

Chapter 10: Welcome the Child

He called a little child: Matthew 18:2–3

Therefore, whoever humbles himself like this child: Matthew 18:4–6, 10–14

Then little children were brought to Jesus: Matthew 19:13–15

What good thing must I do: Matthew 19:16

Then come, follow me: Matthew 19:21

Who then can be saved: Matthew 19:25

With man this is impossible: Matthew 19:26

My house will be called a house of prayer: Matthew 21:13

The blind and the lame came to him: Matthew 21:14–16

The kingdom of heaven belongs to such as these: Matthew 19:14

Chapter 11: Alive in a Million Mysteries

Look at the birds of the air: Matthew 6:26

[Christ is] the firstborn over all creation: Colossians 1:15–17

[Your Father] causes his sun to rise: Matthew 5:45

Look at the birds of the air: Matthew 6:26

See how the lilies of the field grow: Matthew 6:28

In the beginning: Genesis 1:1

Let there be light: Genesis 1:3

He was with God in the beginning: John 1:2–4

He was in the world: John 1:10–13

Speak up for those who cannot: Proverbs 31:8

Chapter 12: Stamp of Empire

Where your treasure is: Matthew 6:21

The kingdom is like a merchant: Matthew 13:45–46

All the believers were one in heart and mind: Acts 4:32–35

When Jesus had finished saying these things: Matthew 7:28
No one can serve two masters: Matthew 6:24

Chapter 13: We Must Go Through Many Hardships

Blessed are you when men hate you: Luke 6:22–23
They stoned Paul and dragged him outside the city: Acts
    14:19–22
We must go through many hardships: Acts 14:22
With healing in [His] wings: Malachi 4:2

Chapter 14: Slow Train Coming

Then I saw a new heaven and a new earth: Revelation
    21:1–4
Rejoice in that day and leap for joy: Luke 6:23
Because great is your reward in heaven: Luke 6:23
All of creation groans: see Romans 8:22
Now the dwelling of God is with men: Revelation 21:3–4
One thing I ask of the LORD: Psalm 27:4
Fruit trees that bear every month, not just once a year: see
    Revelation 22:2
For the joy set before him endured the cross: Hebrews 12:2
Coming down out of heaven from God: Revelation 21:2
We know that when he appears: 1 John 3:2–3

WORKS CITED

Chapter 6: Jesus' Kingdom of Peace

J. R. R. Tolkien, *The Silmarillion,* ed. Christopher Tolkien (Boston:
    Allen & Unwin, 1977).

Chapter 11: Alive in a Million Mysteries

Eugene Peterson's story of Sister Lychen: Eugene H. Peterson, *Christ Plays in Ten Thousand Places: A Conversation in Spiritual Theology* (Grand Rapids: Eerdmans, 1995), 65–71.

Chapter 12: Stamp of Empire

Jubilee celebration: Shane Claiborne, *The Irresistible Revolution: Living as an Ordinary Radical* (Grand Rapids: Zondervan, 2006), 187.

Chapter 14: Slow Train Coming

Assumptions about heaven: Randy Alcorn, *Heaven* (Wheaton, IL: Tyndale, 2004).

Bob Dylan's first gospel album: "Slow Train" and "When He Returns," Bob Dylan, *Slow Train Coming* [sound recording] (New York: Columbia, 1979).

Also by Rick McKinley:

Jesus in the Margins
Reimagine Your Life

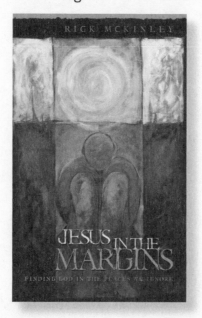

Jesus is our ultimate model for finding identity, acceptance, and legitimacy from the Father. He can identify with life in the margins because when God came to earth in the person of Jesus Christ, He landed in the margins. On purpose. And He chose to land there because it's in the margins that broken lives get mended, prisoners are set free, and the poor hear the Good News.